Real, Raw, & Relatable

Real, Raw, & Relatable

Corporate Badass Mom to Zen Mom

TRISH PERRY

First Edition
ISBN: 978-1-955541-05-3

Library of Congress Control Number: 2022916262

Cover and Interior Design by Ann Aubitz
Photos by AdobeStock and from the collection of Trish Perry
unless otherwise noted.

Published by FuzionPress
1250 E 115th Street
Burnsville, MN 55337
Fuzionpress.com
612-781-2815

CONTENTS

	My Journey	9
1	The Corporate Badass Mom - CBAM	14
2	Dear Cancer	18
3	#MeToo	22
4	A Horse is a Horse of Course of Course	28
5	Ah, Southern Cooking	32
6	When was the Last Time You…	36
7	Do I Dial 911?	40
8	Breast Cancer CAN be a Laughing Matter	44
9	Divorce Over Mustard?	48
10	Hold me Closer Tony Danza	54
11	"Fatty Patty 2x4"	58
12	Visiting Hours in heaven	64
13	Rehearsal Dinner	68

14	How Bad Could it Be? BAD!	74
15	I am an Addict	78
16	Chest or Breast	82
17	Mom Bangs	86
18	Resilient in Neon Pink	94
19	SHOTGUN!	100
20	I'm Sorry, What's Your Name?	106
21	No STOP!	110
22	Oh, Gross!	118
23	Oh, No, Jan Brady!	122
24	It's My Fault!	128
25	More Mama, More!	132
26	Perspective From a Pink Stationwagon	136
27	Quitters vs. Survivors?	142
28	"I Will NOT Be Held Hostage!"	146
29	Does Grief Have a Shelf Life?	152
30	If You Were a Tree…	158
31	I'll Be Happy When…	166
32	Katie an' Da Beas' vs. Bucky Beaver	170
33	The Deep End	174
34	Passion vs. Image	180
35	True Leadership	186
36	Vanity vs. Reality	190
37	Planning Divorce Before Marriage?	196
38	Brutal Honesty	200
39	Unlikely Friends	204

40	The Guest House	208
41	Hired at Eight Months Pregnant?!	214
42	Facebook and Grief	218
43	The Drunken Baby Walk!	222
44	Call the Coast Guard	228
45	Reality TV and Chocolate	232
46	Soul Soother	238
47	Action Figures	244
48	SNOW!	248
49	I am SO Lazy!	252
50	An Act of Kindness for the Colonel	256
51	If I Could Turn Back Time	260
52	The Making of a 'Zen Mom'	264
	My Destination	269
	Journal Learnings	271
	Review	277
	Gratitude	279
	Who is Trish Perry?	283

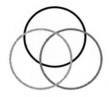

MY JOURNEY

I LOVE LONG, INSIGHTFUL CONVERSATIONS WITH MY KIDS. They remind me what incredible humans my husband and I are lucky enough to parent.

Several years ago, my son Nick and I were in one of those conversations.

Nick: "I am really lucky that I've had two moms."

Me: "Uh, no, I guarantee you've only had one. I have the scars to prove it!"

Nick: "No, you don't understand. When I was younger, you were a Corporate Badass Mom. We learned a lot, like our work ethic, tenacity, negotiations, and how to stand up for ourselves and others. But it was hard—really hard. Remember high school?"

Me: I shuddered, remembering our countless arguments. "Yes, unfortunately, I do, and I am sorry I was so hard on you."

Nick: "Yeah, but now we have a 'Zen Mom'!"

Me: "What? What do you mean a 'Zen Mom'?"

Nick: "It happened when you had cancer and left corporate. This is you being a 'Zen Mom' right now. You are talking *with* me, not *at* me...."

See, isn't he an amazing human? In a single conversation, Nick gave me insight that changed my world. It was then that I realized that breast cancer saved my life: not physically but emotionally, mentally, and spiritually! The Corporate Badass Mom road was leading me down a destructive path!

As a CBAM—Corporate Badass Mom—life was all about being the best. Life was about perfection and impressions.

You see, I was raised by a full-bird colonel. My dad had unrealistic expectations of his children, much like we were his troops. He expected that we respect and obey him, follow the rules (even though they were never laid out), get outstanding grades, work through high school, go to college, get a good job, get married, have kids, etc.

There was no room for failure, no room for questioning, no room for vulnerability. In fact, vulnerability was a four-letter word. *Weak* was how I was raised to view vulnerability. So as a CBAM, I never showed vulnerability—that would mean I was *weak*.

And then, a series of adversities rocked my world, and there was no choice but to accept help from others and to be vulnerable. Those adversities included having a double mastectomy to remove breast cancer, my father having brain surgery, my sister dying of cancer, and caring for my dad through dementia; all of these in a nine-month period. I had to ask for and accept help. I shared my stories with family, friends, peers, and even strangers. Vulnerability is actually my Superpower now.

Vulnerability makes me more relatable and opens up conversations that would otherwise be left unspoken.

Vulnerability has also allowed me to write newsletters and now publish this book, two things I never thought I'd ever do. Acceptance of my own vulnerability is what allowed me to evolve from a CBAM into a 'Zen Mom'

Real, Raw, & Relatable is a collection of my weekly newsletters. My weekly newsletters tell the story of my life followed by the insights, revelations, and lessons I've learned. They are meant to shine a light on those things we hide from ourselves and others, like grief, failure, fear, and self-deprecation. And it is meant to celebrate things like change, humor, positive mindset, and joy.

Craig Neal, coach extraordinaire and the founder of the Center for Purposeful Leadership, emailed me in 2021, "I do love your postings...real, raw, and relatable!" Thus, the title of this book. Thank you, Craig!

Please join me in my stories. I invite you to reflect on how the themes of these stories show up in your life. I wrote this as if we were having a conversation in my living room.

I encourage you to take your time reading this book. Savor it. Journal with each story and talk to friends and family about your thoughts. I've included journaling questions, activities, and challenges at the end of each story, as well as a downloadable journal, which is my gift to you for purchasing this book. You can download the journal at **https:/harmonizeu.com/rrrjournal/**.

Thanks to each and every one of you for being willing to read about my journey and reflect on your own journey along the way. I've retired from my CBAM days; my journey as a 'Zen Mom' continues to evolve. Each of these stories is a part of my journey…

Enjoy!

My family, my loves, my joy!

#1
The Corporate Badass Mom
CBAM

Me, the CBAM in 2009

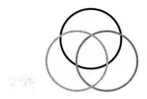

CLICK, CLICK, CLICK... "OH, SHIT NICK, YOUR MOM'S HERE!"

That *click, click, click* was the sound of my heels hitting the high school's concrete floor. Somehow my kids and their friends knew the sound of my purposeful walk. They also knew that if I was headed to their classroom, it couldn't be good news.

I found out just how hurtful that *click, click, click* was during that conversation with my son a few years ago.

Remember where my journey began? Where my son shared that I went from a CBAM to 'Zen Mom'?

Well, during his high school years I was full CBAM.

Yes, I remembered high school; it was one big argument. I remember trying to control everything—literally everything: my job, my home, my kids, my husband, everything! For my kids and my husband, I am sure this was pure hell.

My thoughts as a CBAM? If I could control everything, life would be perfect. I would be successful, and I would never fail.

Our fixation on "success" and "failure" is really a trap.

My fixation on success caused me to behave in ways I'm embarrassed about today.

If things were not perfect, I'd yell at my kids and my husband. And just as bad, I'd yell at myself! I'd yell at the waitstaff at a restaurant if we had to wait too long or if the service was bad. I'd yell at salespeople if the lines were too long or if they would not give me credit for an item I was trying to return. It's embarrassing, but true.

This entire book could be about my bad behavior, but the purpose of the book is to tell you about the transformation of my bad behavior, mindset, and life!

Once I let go of control and perfection, and the fear of failure, my life changed dramatically; I became a 'Zen Mom'. My son beautifully illustrated the change in our short conversation.

Please download your complimentary journal to reflect on your own journey throughout this book. https://harmonizeu.com.

Journaling Questions:

1. When have you been fixated on success and fear of failure in your life?
2. What effects did this have on you, your family, your friends, your relationships, your work, and your life?
3. What have you done to change your mindset?
4. If you haven't changed your mindset yet, please continue reading the book for ideas on this and journal what resonates with you.

#2
Dear
Cancer

THIS IS THE 10-YEAR ANNIVERSARY OF MY DOUBLE MASTECTOMY.

I wrote the letter below three years after my surgery, when I realized I was chronically sad and mad about my breast cancer. Oh, and the fact that within a year of my own cancer, both my sister and best friend died of cancer.

Instead of staying angry, I chose to look at the gifts in my life, and this letter was the result. Cancer and death led to a change in mindset and saved my life!

Dear Cancer,

As unusual as this may seem, this is a thank you letter.

Do you cause pain and suffering? Yes, and I hate you for that.

What you don't realize is that through all of the pain and suffering comes endless love, pure compassion, wonderful and meaningful friendships, endless kindness that is magnified beyond imagination, and an appreciation for people so deep that it is indescribable! This was never your intention—so you don't win.

You took my sister, you took my friends, and you tried to take me, but you still don't win. You see, I ended up more in love, more alive, more gentle, more peaceful, and more appreciative. So again, you don't win!

My children have seen such deep love and gratitude that they wouldn't otherwise have seen. They have experienced a way of seeing life that I could not teach them. So again, you don't win.

You have given me wonderful opportunities, like participating in the three-day breast cancer walk with friends. We have such great memories of the fun, the laughter, the support, the bonding, and the strength that was built through that experience. So again, you don't win.

You have changed me. I am a better mother, sister, friend, wife, and person than I was without your presence in my life. So again, you don't win.

So Cancer, in a strange way I have to say thank you—you do not win, I do!

Journaling Questions and Activity:

1. What have you been mad, sad, or resentful about that is affecting your life in negative ways?
2. Write two letters; you won't send them. I suggest that you burn them. If you can't burn them, then tear them up and bury them outside.
   a. Write an "f-you" letter about the situation or person. Let it go. How do you really feel? Get it out of your head, heart, and soul and onto paper.
   b. Now, write a thank you letter about the situation or to the person. What are the lessons you have learned? How has this situation changed you for the better?
3. Read both of your letters out loud, then burn them in a fire pit, a grill, or even a fire-proof bowl. Be sure to have water on hand to put out the fire! Or tear them up and bury your letters outside.
4. How did it feel to read those letters and then let them go? You can do this with as many situations or people as you'd like!
5. Once you've done this, notice how you feel. Journal this and continue to let go… for YOURSELF, not for others.

#3
#MeToo

*"When one person says,
'Yeah, me, too,' it gives
permission for
others to open up."*
~Tarana Burke

W hat do Alyssa Milano, Reese Witherspoon, Jennifer Lawrence, Gwyneth Paltrow, Trish Perry, and Tarana Burke have in common?

WAIT, WHO IS TARANA BURKE?

#MeToo is the common thread between all of these women. Tarana Burke was the originator of the Me Too movement in 2006. Burke started it to empower vulnerable women, mainly women of color, around sexual harassment and abuse. She had no idea that in October of 2017, it would become THE social movement and national outcry for women who had experienced sexual abuse.

In 2017, after Harvey Weinstein had been accused of sexual assault and abuse by several women, Alyssa Milano tweeted, "If you've been sexually harassed or assaulted, write 'me too' as a reply to this tweet." In 45 days, 85 million people replied to or shared this tweet! Milano had no idea that Tarana Burke had actually started this movement, so Burke initially was not credited.

Was Tarana Burke upset that a celebrity, especially a White woman, had stolen her idea? Initially, yes, but then she looked at it with a new lens. Instead of viewing Alyssa Milano as a thief, she viewed her as a vessel, a catalyst. Burke has since worked with Milano to broaden the movement and ensure women of color, men, trans, and all people are included.

Speaking as a fellow #MeToo woman, I held onto my pain and resentment and didn't look through a different lens for over 40 years. Being sexually abused at five, I pushed the reality out of my conscious brain until I was 40. Once I admitted the abuse, it took me over 10 years to realize that I wasn't "damaged" and that I hadn't done anything to warrant the abuse.

Becoming a coach helped me look at the situation through a different lens. I am stronger and I can help others in a more successful way. I no longer think the abuse was my fault, and I am at peace with my situation. I am so thankful for having a different view of my abuse.

We all have had situations that seem unfair or painful. Thoughts run through our minds: "I can't believe I didn't get credit for that," "This is so unfair," "I'll show them," "It's my fault, I'm not good enough," or "I just can't handle this." These thoughts ruminate in our brains and cause us to become stuck, getting in the way of our peace of mind.

But what if you looked at your situation through a different lens?

When Burke put a new lens on her situation, she realized that her initial mission of giving Black women a way to share their stories and promoting the idea of empathy through empowerment could not only be fulfilled, it could expand.

Had Burke kept the resentment and anger that her idea was "stolen," she would not have worked with celebrities like Gabrielle Union to ensure Black women weren't shut out of the movement. She would not have worked with Milano and Terry Crews to expand the movement, mission, and action that is "bigger than her," as she said.

#MeToo is now a worldwide movement. Burke is now known as the originator and is living her mission in a much bigger way. Holding on to her resentment and anger would have been detrimental to this success.

Journaling Questions:

Note, if you have experienced abuse, seeking a mental health professional to help to process the abuse is recommended.

1. What resentment or anger are you holding on to in your life?
2. Where could you use a different lens to view a seemingly unfair or painful situation?
3. How can you use this different view to change your mindset?
4. Go back to story 2. Would it help you to write letters to get a different mindset?
5. How has the #MeToo movement affected you and your life?

CONSIDERATIONS ON #MeToo...

"If you light a lantern for another, it will also brighten your own way..."
~Nichiren

"One moment can change a day, one day can change a life and one life can change the world..."
~Gautama The Lord Buddha

"After the verb 'to love,' 'to help' is the most beautiful verb in the world."
~Bertha von Suttner

#4
A Horse Is a Horse of Course of Course

Art by Kris https://www.artpal.com/knormanmajor

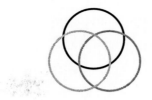

THE TITLE OF THIS STORY IS THE LYRICS FROM A 1960S
SHOW FEATURING A TALKING HORSE, MR. ED. This
was one of my favorite shows. Growing up, I
watched the reruns weekly.

Maybe it was because I also knew a talking horse,
though her name was Jane, not Mr. Ed.

Jane was a beautiful, gentle brown horse with eyes
that you got lost in! I swear she talked to my Uncle Jack.
Summers in North Carolina, we spent long glorious days
at the barn riding and talking to Jane.

Jane and Uncle Jack had conversations about me. He
told her that "Yankees" weren't lucky enough to spend
time with horses. He'd asked her to be on her best behavior.
Then he'd throw his head back, laugh, and say, "I hear
you, Jane, you're always on your best behavior. I love you
so." He would kiss her, and she would nuzzle him for
what seemed like hours.

Jane brought Uncle Jack a joy that can't be described
in words.

I want that joy! One of my goals is to find that same joy that Uncle Jack found with Jane.

What brings me joy? Family, friends, coaching, helping people, etc. Then a friend challenged me: "Trish, I get it, but I what brings YOU joy—just you, without others." That is a harder question to answer, and I am working on it.

What brings *you* joy? It's an important question to answer. Joy is wonderful in good times and it is necessary in bad times. Joy helps us work through adversities. It helps us to have hope in otherwise hopeless situations.

A friend of mine found joy painting with alcohol inks in 2020 and loves it.

Then, the unspeakable happened, her daughter died by suicide. It has been a time filled with grief, sadness, and deep pain.

Her painting brings her joy and that joy gives her respite from the grief and pain. She is able to rebuild her reserves to go on. The joy *helps* her to grieve.

This painting, pictured after the title, is one of her beautiful, joyful pieces.

So, I ask again, what brings *you* joy? *Everyone* deserves joy. *Everyone*!

Journaling Questions:

1. What do you enjoy doing, even if you are not an expert at it?
2. What activity makes you forget time? Forget to eat? Forget the world while you are doing it?
3. What brings you joy? If you don't know, try things—a lot of things, even things you haven't done before. Make it a goal to find what brings you joy.
4. How will you bring more joy into your life? Be specific and put dates to it!

#5
Ah, Southern Cooking

My mom making biscuits

M

Y MOM WAS A *GREAT* SOUTHERN COOK!
But she didn't start out that way.
Like the time she made biscuits with water.
Any Southern mama knows that you use buttermilk or milk, but she was not a mama...yet.

Mom put the biscuits in the oven and set the timer. The timer went off, she opened the oven, and there were the most glorious golden-brown biscuits she'd ever seen. "I declare," she marveled at her creation.

She proudly presented them to her nieces and nephews. She didn't realize the water had turned her biscuits into hockey pucks. The kids bit into them and yelled, "Aunt Betty, we can't even eat these!"

So, what do you do with the food you can't eat? In the South, you give it to the chickens. But the biscuits were so hard that even the chickens couldn't eat them. The biscuits were a failure!

To her credit, my mom didn't label herself a failure as a cook. She asked for help from her sister, found her mistake, and made a great batch of biscuits the next week.

She eventually became an excellent Southern cook through trial and error. She asked for help, tested, adjusted, and voilà, a fabulous Southern cook! My friends were so jealous because their moms couldn't cook as she did.

Her failures did not define her!

How many of us have failed at something and stopped trying? We let that failure define us.

My failure story? I couldn't climb the rope in gym class. Kids were mean. It was embarrassing and hurtful, so I started saying, "I'm sorry, I was born without an athletic gene." Nine out of ten times, the teachers found it funny, so I didn't have to participate. I defined myself as a nonathletic person because of one failure: the inability to climb a rope.

Am I now an Olympic athlete? No, but I kickbox two times a week. Not the MMA kind, but the YouTube video for fitness kind. It's fun and involves all kinds of athletic moves.

I'm also a bike rider, a walker, a snow-shoer, and a weightlifter, now and then. All require some athletic prowess.

So, guess what? It wasn't that I was born without an athletic gene, it was just covered up for a few years!

Journaling Questions:

1. Do you have a failure that is defining you? If so, what is it?
2. Think about the failure. What was the reason for the failure? How can you change your mindset so it doesn't define you?
3. What do you currently do in your life where you have had failures yet you still do that activity? (E.g., cooking, art, playing an instrument, sports, etc.)
4. How does it feel to continue these activities even if you aren't an expert?

#6
When Was the Last Time You...

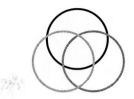

MY CLIENT, MARY, WAS ALL SMILES. "I received fifty red roses, a gift card, and a note that said, 'You are worth it.' *It felt so good.*"

Mary was newly divorced and had been going through some really *rough* times.

"Wow, who sent them to you?" I asked.

"I did! I decided I wanted roses for Valentine's Day, so *I sent them to myself.*"

I was speechless and *so* proud of her. She had come so far in six months!

My hope is that each one of us can embrace self-love like Mary did, even after going through tough adversities that make us question ourselves.

Mary had someone in her life who knew her incredible gifts, knew how special she was, and knew she was worth it; she has *herself!*

We often wait for someone else to make us feel good when, in fact, we already have someone with us 24/7 who can make us feel good. That someone in your life…is *you.* When was the last time you bought or sent yourself a gift?

Do you see your own self-worth? Do you have the self-love to prioritize yourself? We are sometimes our own worst enemy, but Mary proved that we can also be our own best advocate.

There is an effective assignment on self-worth that I give to my clients like Mary. I'd like to share it with you.

Create a list of 100 positive "I am…" statements. The key is that you will write some of these yourself, but also ask family members, friends, and coworkers to help you. You have to accept all of their positive statements because this is how they experience you, even if you don't see it in yourself. If you have a hard time asking, blame it on me: "I've been given a challenge by a coach to write a hundred positive "I am" statements and to ask family, friends, and coworkers to help. I'd appreciate it if you could give me some feedback on what some of my "I am" statements should be. Thanks so much!"

Examples are, "I am strong," "I am compassionate," "I am a great friend," "I am strategic," "I am an artist," "I am a nature lover," etc.

Then sit back and enjoy and bask in your 100 positive statements!

Journaling Questions:

1. When is the last time you sent or bought yourself a gift? Not something you needed, but a true gift?
2. If you haven't bought or sent yourself anything in a while, what would you like? Do you have the self-worth and self-love to buy it and/or send it to yourself?
3. If you don't have the self-worth or self-love, I'd encourage you to complete the "I am" exercise above. It will give you evidence that you ARE worthy!
4. If you did the "I am" exercise, what were some of the most surprising things you received from others or even yourself?
5. How do the "I am" statements make you feel?

#7
Do I Dial 911?

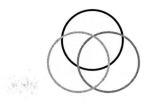

WE WERE HAVING FUN WITH 30 OF OUR NEIGH-BORS...UNTIL I SAW HIM.

Walking down the sidewalk was a clean-cut man, well dressed in a baseball hat, a hoodie, and jeans. Well, he was actually stumbling and weaving, not walking, down the sidewalk.

He was obviously *very* high or drunk. And then he fell—hard!

Do I dial 911?

Living in Minneapolis with George Floyd's murder fresh in mind, I hesitated. The man was Black. He didn't need to be arrested; he needed help.

He got back up and fell again; he was in distress.

I did not want to fail him or myself by being a by-stander or just calling for help for my own safety.

I dialed 911 and pleaded with them to send EMTs, not the police. He wasn't a criminal and needed medical help.

We waited and heard sirens. The man panicked. The sirens stopped, he relaxed, and then we saw ambulance lights.

I flagged the ambulance down in front of our house where the man stood wavering.

The EMTs were so gentle and kind to him. He put his head on the EMT's chest and then collapsed. Putting him on the gurney, he passed out immediately.

The ambulance stayed for about 20 minutes. Someone suggested that they might be administrating Narcan.

Whatever they were doing, this man wouldn't go to jail; he would be taken to the hospital to get help.

I was so relieved and thankful that this didn't go a different way had they sent the police.

What helped me make my decision? The three core questions I use when making decisions or setting goals are:

1. **What values does my decision align with?** Getting help for this man aligned with my values of love, integrity, and compassion, but only if they sent an ambulance. I had to take the chance, as this man obviously needed help.
2. **What will I have if I make this decision?** I'd have peace of mind that this man received help, but if they sent police and shot him, I would have a life full of guilt. I had to take the chance, as this man obviously needed help.
3. **How will my life be different if I make this decision?** I'd know that I helped someone. My intent

was to help, not to harm. I would feel guilty if I did nothing, and I would feel guilty if the police came and hurt him. I had to take the chance, this man needed help.

I'm thankful I asked these questions. I don't know what happened to that man *and* I feel good about my decision.

Journaling Questions:

1. Have you made decisions in the past that were difficult for you to make?
2. What are your core values? These are the top five or six values that help you make decisions and help you live your life authentically.
3. Think about a hard decision you had to make. What criteria did you use to make the decision?
4. Do you have a decision you have to make in the near future? Be sure to use your values to help decide.

#8
Breast Cancer CAN Be a Laughing Matter

Nick, 17, Hannah, 15, and Riley, 12…laughing

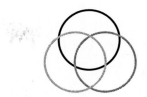

W E CALLED OUR KIDS INTO THE LIVING ROOM, then ages 17, 15, and 12.

They sat quietly listening and waiting for the family meeting. They wondered what they had done now. The dread in the room was palpable.

This was a serious family issue and we had to make a decision, as a family. I had been diagnosed with breast cancer. "Should I have a single or a double mastectomy?" I fought back the tears, the words fresh on my tongue.

Our oldest, Nicholas, said, "Double, definitely double. You know how you are about symmetry, Mama."

Swiftly following her brother, Hannah, our 15-year-old, said with a straight face, "Yeah, double. Mama, do you really want one Victoria's Secret boob and one mom boob?"

Our 12-year-old, Riley, laughed and agreed that a double was the decision.

We all laughed in unison. "Bartender, I'll take a double!"

And there it was, out of the mouths of babes, the two comments that quite possibly saved my life.

The dread was swiftly replaced with humor and the tears were lifted to laughter. The comments brought joy to an otherwise scary situation.

Breast cancer was, in fact, a laughing matter.

You see, these comments did not change our circumstances. These comments gave us the power to choose humor and love over dread and bitterness.

This is a very powerful tool in my coaching practice. Everyone *deserves* joy, regardless of their circumstances.

In our case, we chose joy vs. dread. The joy that our amazing children created. Jay and I, as adults, initially saw this as sadness. Wow, children are wonderful teachers!

Journaling Questions:

1. Have you ever had a hard time choosing joy over sadness or bitterness?
2. What did you do or what caused you to choose joy over sadness or bitterness?
3. If you were able to choose a different mindset, what were the results?
4. Think about a time when you wish you would have chosen joy. How would your situation have changed?
5. What can you do in the future to make a choice of joy or even neutrality vs. feeling like you have to live with sadness, bitterness, or resentment?

#9
Divorce over Mustard?

YEP, I ALMOST DIVORCED JAY ON OUR HONEYMOON
32 YEARS AGO, OVER MUSTARD!
Imagine a romantic boat ride on Lake Tahoe.

Two newlyweds in love decide to get a snack. Hot dogs and chips are the only fares, but they like hot dogs.

In fact, when Jay and I lived in Louisiana, we always got Lucky Dogs in New Orleans after hours. We'd search out the only cart that carried ketchup for my hot dogs. Sometimes it took an hour.

Jay knew I only liked ketchup, never mustard, so we persevered to find that lone cart that carried ketchup in all of the French Quarter.

Fast forward, and here we were, newly married, on our honeymoon and a romantic boat ride. Jay proudly walked back to me, holding two hot dogs covered in what? MUSTARD!

I lost it! You would have thought he'd had an affair.

I know this sounds over the top, but right then, those hotdogs symbolized our relationship. If he couldn't re-member the ketchup, then he must not love me.

Huh?

I was like a toddler who didn't get her way. It was an amygdala hijack.

The amygdala, that survival part of our brain that controls fight, flight, or freeze, was in control. And I was in fight mode.

Really, over a hot dog?

In my 20s, I didn't even know the amygdala existed, let alone what the amygdala did.

How could I have known to take a deep breath and allow my executive brain, my prefrontal cortex, to come online and reason through this minor misstep?

Does this sound familiar?

Not the divorce over mustard, but being hijacked by your amygdala? Have you ever lost it with a spouse, a child, a peer, a boss, or an employee, only to regret it later?

As a coach, I now have the tools to learn to calm the amygdala and allow response vs. reaction.

Reacting is what the amygdala does. Responding is what the prefrontal cortex does.

The latter is much more effective and successful for relationships.

Journaling Questions and Tools:

1. When you get upset or scared, do you let yourself react or do you have the tools to get to respond mode?
2. Think about a time when you got angry and said something or did something that you regretted.
3. What was your reaction? Were you in amygdala hijack?
4. How could you have settled your brain enough to respond vs. react?

Tools:

Here are three tools you can use to respond vs. react. These tools will help you get out of amygdala hijack.

1. Rub your thumb and index finger together very lightly. Pay close attention to what you feel. Can you feel the ridges of your fingerprint? Doing this helps you come back to the present moment.
2. Take a walk, go up and down the steps, or run in place. This helps your body to get rid of the stress hormone, cortisol, that sent your amygdala into fight flight or freeze and helps you settle down.
3. Take five deep breaths. Pay attention to your chest and abdomen expanding and contracting. Continue the breaths until you can fully feel the expansion and contraction in your body. You are

becoming present and this will allow you to think about how you want to respond vs. reacting in the moment.

CONSIDERATIONS ON REACTING VS. RESPONDING...

"Do not learn how to react. Learn how to respond."
~Gautama The Lord Buddha

"Life is ten percent what happens to you and ninety percent how you respond to it."
~Lou Holtz

"Be thoughtful and mindful about the things you say to other people..."
~Evan Spiegel

#10

Hold Me Closer Tony Danza

Misheard Lyrics

"Hold me closer Tony Danza"
"Money for nothin' and your chips for free"
"Dancing queen, feel the beat from the tangerine"
"We built this city; we built this city on sausage rolls"
"Excuse me while I kiss this guy"
"Sweet dreams are made of cheese"
"I can see clearly now, Lorraine is gone"
"Kickin' your cat all over the place"
"Don't go Jason Waterfalls"
"I like big butts in a can of limes"

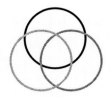

I WAS BORN WITH A DEFICIENT GENE...A DEFICIENT LYRIC GENE!

Can you name the song from these lyrics that I misheard?

1. "She's got electric boots, a mohasooze, you know I read it, and I'm back insane"
2. "Carry a laser down the road that I must travel"

Well, the first set is from "Bennie and the Jets" by Elton John. The actual lyrics are "She's got leather boots, a mohair suit, you know I read it in a magazine."

The second set is from "Kyrie Eleison" by Mr. Mister. The actual lyrics are "Kyrie Eleison, down the road that I must travel."

See, I'm lyric deficient. I often hear lyrics differently than the artist sings.

I have a choice: I can either be embarrassed or laugh. Actually, I not only laugh, I choose to be vulnerable and bring humor to people through my mistakes.

You see, I often write about my lyric gaffes on Facebook.

People make comments like, "I just love reading about your misheard lyrics, it makes me laugh. Thank you!"

So, let's break this down: the artists were trying to tell a story, I misheard their words, found out the correct lyrics, then make people laugh by telling my tales.

I'd say that is a win!

In my teen and early adult years, this kind of gaffe would cause an amazing amount of embarrassment.

I never would have admitted it, let alone broadcast it on Facebook! Everyone would make fun of me!

In fact, instead of embarrassment, I now choose vulnerability. It is very freeing, it makes me more relatable, creates connections with others, and people often share stories of their own.

I consider vulnerability a power tool. We all have a set of tools or skills that we use in our lives. What is your power tool or power skill?

P.S. And no, those lyrics of the title story aren't correct. "Hold me closer Tony Danza" isn't about the famous actor from *Who's the Boss*. It is, of course, the lyrics to the Elton John song "Tiny Dancer": "Hold me closer tiny dancer."

Journaling Questions and Challenge:

1. How do you feel about vulnerability in your life?
2. How have you used vulnerability?
3. What was the outcome?
4. Power Path Challenge: If you shy away from vulnerability because you think it makes you weak, I challenge you to try vulnerability to connect with people instead. At least one time this month, try it out and send me an email to let me know how it went.

#11
"Fatty Patty 2 X 4"

Me in third grade

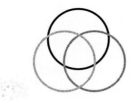

"FATTY PATTY TWO-BY-FOUR CAN'T FIT THROUGH THE CLASSROOM DOOR."

Simon, the meanest boy in third grade, decided that I would be his target that week. He made fun of my hair, outfits, shoes, anything. None of it bothered me.

Until he landed on my soft, vulnerable spot. I hated the nickname Patty. But he zeroed in on what rhymed with Fatty, and so it began.

Yes, that is me in third grade. I loved that outfit. My mom made it for me, and I remember carefully picking out the butterfly fabric and the Simplicity Pattern. Every morning I'd ask my mom, "Is it done yet?"

Finally, the night before picture day, it was complete. I tried it on, and it was perfection! I felt like Cheryl Tiegs (a 1970s supermodel). "Thank you, Mom. I LOVE it! I'm wearing it tomorrow!"

I thought the third grade was off to a great start.

Then, on picture day, Simon started singing, "Fatty Patty two-by-four, can't fit through the classroom door!" I heard this at least 100 times that week. The next week he moved on to his next victim and I was free from the chant.

But the damage was done. That one comment, sung 100 times, became indelibly imprinted on my brain. My inner critic latched onto "Fatty Patty," and I forever became the fat girl.

I went on a diet that year, third grade, and lost five pounds. This started the life of yo-yo weight loss and gain.

I've lost and gained hundreds of pounds in my life, and I never lost the internal stamp of "Fatty Patty." Look at my picture—I was far from fat. But that comment from a mean boy when I was eight became my identity.

I was letting my inner critic navigate my life.

Who is an inner critic? An inner critic is the negative voice in your head that tells you you're not good enough.

"Fatty Patty two-by-four" was one of the strongest messages for my inner critic.

Fast forward 40+ years. I was in a learning session at my coaching school, Learning Journeys, and I uncovered my inner critic. I was stunned. Do you mean all of those negative voices were not mine? No, they weren't. To further emphasize that, we were instructed to give our inner critic a name and an image. This was powerful for me!

That was the day that I started dealing with "Fatty Patty," and my inner critic.

Meet "The Colonel," my inner critic. His image is his finger pointing in judgment.

Every time I hear that "Fatty Patty" message, I imagine that finger pointing in my face and I say, "Not today, Colonel," to quiet him.

It takes a *long* time to quiet those messages.

In my case, "Fatty Patty" has taken me six years to quiet. Since identifying The Colonel I have to keep on top of it because the thought continues, albeit less often and not as loud. I have to say, "No thank you, not today," and go on with my day without "Fatty Patty" playing over and over in my mind.

Hard work? Yes. Worth it? Absolutely!

Journaling Questions:

1. What messages does your inner critic consistently say in your mind?
2. Have you been able to quiet that negative voice?
3. Do you have a name or an image for those negative messages? For example, mine is "The Colonel," and his image is a finger pointing in my face.
4. How has your inner critic affected your life? Has it stopped you from living life to its fullest?
5. How can you quiet your inner critic?

EXAMPLE OF MY INNER CRITIC... "THE COLONEL"

#12
Visiting Hours in Heaven

Walking to visiting hours in heaven

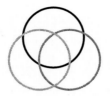

I MISS MY MOM, AND MY SISTER, AND MY DAD AND MY RELATIVES, AND MY FRIENDS, SO...
I've decided to start a petition. A petition to God!

I'd like *visiting hours in heaven*. Just once a year. If that's too much, maybe Zoom calls to heaven? I know, in reality, neither will ever happen.

But I love to think about the long conversations I'd have with my loved ones there.

My loved ones and I would cuddle up on the fluffiest cloud imaginable inside Nordstrom in heaven.

There must be a Nordstrom for my mom and my sister because Nordstrom was their heaven on earth!

I'd bring pictures and stories of my family.

I'd catch them up on everything with a huge smile on my face! They'd smile back knowingly because, of course, they'd been watching every moment from heaven.

I'd ask all kinds of questions about why things happen; they'd smile, and I'd know they couldn't tell me.

We'd hold hands, hug, and laugh until the heavenly bouncers would announce "last call."

Last call for hugs, kisses, laughter, conversation, and whispering "I love you" over and over again!

Again, they'd smile knowingly because they've heard my thoughts every day, and know I love them.

And then it would be time to leave. Tears would stream down my face, I'd know it would be ok, becuase I'd see them again next year!

But I can't have visiting hours or Zoom in heaven, so at least I've found one way to connect with them.

I hold each one of them in my heart. I talk to them, imaging conversations with them. I feel their love in my heart, mind, and soul.

They are always with me…

I guess I don't need visiting hours in heaven after all! (But it would be nice.)

Winnie the Pooh said, "How lucky I am to have something that makes saying goodbye so hard."

I consider myself lucky x 1000!

Journaling Questions and Activity:

1. How do you keep your loved ones you have lost close to you?
2. What is the first thing you'd do if there were visiting hours in heaven?
3. Write down the conversation you'd have with them, in detail.
4. How could you incorporate this into your remembrance of them?

#13
Rehearsal
Dinner

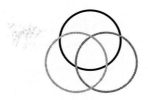

"I RUINED YOUR REHEARSAL DINNER!"

Nicholas, my oldest, tried to soothe me as I sobbed.

"Mama, everyone is having a great time. You did a great job."

On Sunday, March 20, 2022, Nicholas and Kaia had the big wedding and reception that Covid had delayed. It was incredible, beautiful, and an amazing success.

But it was a different story on Saturday night when we hosted 40 people for a rehearsal dinner, or so I thought…

I had been planning this for weeks. I had cooked enough food for 60 people because, well, because that's what I do. I make sure there is enough for everyone to enjoy and even take leftovers if they'd like.

The first person to get dinner was a lovely young man who was sweet and funny *and* had a voracious appetite.

My chest tightened as I watched him take a full one-quarter of the fettuccine alfredo I had made. There would not be enough for everyone! Enter my inner critic, "The Colonel." How could I have miscalculated this badly?

I have lots of tools to fight my inner critic. You know the inner critic? See story eleven if you don't remember.

On Saturday night, he was on active duty. He was yelling about the fact that I hadn't planned well enough and hadn't made enough fettuccine alfredo. I had ruined the party.

As I write this, I realize how ridiculous this sounds.

I even realized it was ridiculous while it was happening, but I was not able to quiet his loud voice in my head. In fact, he just got louder.

I tried to do other things in the kitchen, but he was yelling at me, and I kept making mistakes, including a pan of cookies sliding onto the oven door.

Failure, failure... abort the mission.

I put out the rest of the food and retreated into my bedroom to have a good old-fashioned ugly cry.

Not only had I ruined the party, but I had been rude to people trying to help.

Nicholas gave me the only advice that a coach's son could give.

"You didn't ruin the party. And if you were rude to people, you just apologize. Explain that you were stressed out and that you overreacted. Tell them you really appreciate them and their help and you are sorry. People understand. It'll all be fine."

In fact, both my daughters and my daughter-in-law gave me very similar advice.

In the end, the only way I was able to quiet "The Colonel" was through writing.

I broke the situation down:

1. What were the facts? 1) I had planned the party in detail. 2) There were 40 people at the party. 3) I had made enough food for 60 people. 4) One person had taken a very large serving. 5) There was still a lot of food, for people to eat.

2. What was the story I made up? I should have calculated for someone eating a lot, and I hadn't. How stupid could I be? Not everyone would get fettuccine and would be disappointed. People would think that I should not have hosted the dinner. Nick and Kaia would be very disappointed. I ruined the rehearsal dinner!

3. I read both the facts and the story out loud and asked myself if my story was accurate. It was not! I had blown the situation out of proportion.

With that, I went to the bathroom, put on a new face of makeup, and went back to the party. Guess what? No one even noticed I had left.

Everyone had plenty to eat, plenty to drink, and they were there to celebrate Kaia and Nick, not to criticize the fact that we ran out of fettuccine alfredo. In fact, no one left hungry, *and* there were leftovers.

I hadn't ruined the rehearsal dinner!

Journaling Questions and Activity:

1. Can you relate to this situation? What situation did you blow out of proportion?
2. What were the messages that your inner critic was yelling at you?
3. Write out the situation in the three steps I outlined. The facts, the story you made up, and compare them—what was the reality?
4. How could this method help you in the future?

CONSIDERATION ON STORIES WE MAKE UP...

"That story you are making up in your head about a situation or a person, ask yourself it is based on truth or your perceptions. Take the power out of the story by calling it what it is—made up."
~Trish Perry

"Research shows us that we not only have the capacity to pay attention to and stop the chatter of our stories, but we can also reduce our stress…, and reinvent our relationships by responding to them differently."
~B. Grace Bullock

#14
How Bad Could It Be? BAD!

"Failure is success in progress."

~Albert Einstein

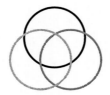

20+ **YEARS AGO,** shortly after moving to Minneapolis for Target, I presented our business plans to Bob Ulrich, the president of Target.

How bad could this be, presenting to the president of Target? Spoiler alert—worse than you'd imagine.

I knew my material backward and forward. I knew I should practice, but I was too embarrassed to practice by myself, let alone in front of my husband or anyone else. And I hated hearing my voice, so I'd never record myself!

So, I relied on memorizing my material. I could answer *any* question anyone asked me. This would be fine, really—it'd be fine, really. Really?

Called into the conference room to meet with Bob, my stomach churned, and I could barely remember my name. I painfully fumbled through the five-minute presentation. My body shook, and my voice shook even more. I could see the winces and cringes on my team's faces.

Remember the question, "How bad could it be?" The answer was…BAD!

I squeaked out a "thank you" and headed straight to the bathroom for the ugly cry that had been just below the surface. I had FAILED!

But that failure is not the end of my presentation story.

In 2021, I gave a 15-minute presentation to AGC, a networking group. It was called "Failing Fearlessly for Success." I gave my presentation to a room of 50+ people. I opened with a failure story that captured my audience, gave examples, asked the audience to help redefine failure, and the presentation ended with applause and an outstanding rating—success!

The difference between the presentations? Experience, a well-timed presentation, practice, practice, more practice, and confidence that came from practice.

I found out in July, 2021 that I was presenting at AGC on September 1st. I immediately started working on the presentation. Several people helped me edit my material. I practiced it in front of my coach and others. I took their ideas and continued to hone my presentation. I practiced on my daily walks, in front of the mirror, in front of my husband, and I practiced in front of my dogs; my best audience by far. I even recorded myself!

It all paid off.

You see, my failure at Target taught me a lot of lessons. As embarrassing as it was, I am thankful for that failure. Sure, I wallowed in my disappointment a little, ok a lot, but then I learned from my mistakes, improved, and tried again.

I have done hundreds of presentations in front of hundreds of people. Now I enjoy it, and dare I say, I am good at it—a far cry from my failed presentation at Target!

Journaling Questions:

1. What are some failures you've had in your life that you can easily remember?
2. What were the lessons that you learned from those failures?
3. How can you use those lessons help you to get better next time?
4. Looking back, how can you be thankful for those-failures?

#15
I am
an Addict

God grant me the serenity
to accept the things I cannot change;
courage to change the things I can;
and wisdom to know the difference.

A shortened version of The Serenity Prayer
~Rienhold Neibuhr

ADMITTING "I AM AN ADDICT" BRINGS UP FEAR. I fear that people will think my addiction is alcohol or drugs.

And what if it is/was? My addiction is just that, an addiction. The difference is that some addictions, like mine, are "socially acceptable."

My addiction is to achieving. In fact, my worth is tied to achieving. I am what Shirzad Chamine, author of *Positive Intelligence*, calls a hyper-achiever. It doesn't matter how much I have to do; I take on more.

The hidden reason I overextend is that it makes me feel worthy. I thought I overextended because I like to be busy and I like to help. The insidious part of the hyper-achiever is that when you strip it down, it is about feeling worthy. It hurts to feel worthless.

In 2012, I came face to face with my addiction. I had a double mastectomy. My doctor said I would be out for at least six weeks.

Six weeks? No way! Instead, I searched the web to find evidence that I could do it in less time. Eureka! A woman who had a single mastectomy went back to work in two weeks. I set my goal for three weeks. I added an additional week for my other breast. Smart, right? WRONG!

After one week, I was in so much pain I could barely walk. How was I going to get to work? *Nope, don't think that way, stick to your goal*, I thought. *I'll be back to work in two more weeks.*

You guessed it; I was out for six weeks. I went into a deep depression. In my mind, healing didn't count as achieving anything. To me, healing wasn't an active achievement. I had missed my three-week goal.

I went back to work feeling like a failure. I pushed myself too hard, trying to prove my worth, and ended up back in bed. Yep, fear of failure had a tight grip on me!

Then the universe intervened. My sister was diagnosed with stage 4 cancer. I immediately quit my job to be with her. I didn't even think about achievement! My only thoughts were helping her to heal and being with her.

She died eight weeks later. Again, I did not have one thought about lack of achievement; I was focused on losing her.

It was in her death that I realized my addiction. I realized how much I had focused on the present in the past few weeks; when I wasn't worried about achieving. I was focused on really *being* with my sister in those final weeks.

Admitting and accepting that you have a problem is the first step to addiction recovery. I have been on and off the recovery wagon for nine years.

I have found ways to interrupt my thoughts of worthlessness by connecting to my achievements. I ask myself if my worth is tied to the number of projects I am working on. If so, I acknowledge it and loosen the reigns.

I also say mantras every morning, "I matter, and what I offer the world matters, regardless of achievement," and "I forgive myself for any mistakes I've made."

These mantras and others remind me of my worth, no matter my achievements. They also remind me that making mistakes is a part of life. Failure is not fatal; in fact, it's part of success!

Journaling Questions:

1. Do you have a "socially acceptable" addiction? Are you a workaholic? A perfectionist? Are you addicted to caffeine, the internet, shopping, exercise, or adrenaline?
2. What impact does your addiction have on your life?
3. Have you acknowledged your addiction?
4. What is one small step you could take to curb your addiction?

#16
Chest or Breast?

"Words can inspire.
And words can destroy.
Choose yours well."
~Robin Sharma

"There is power in words.
What you say is what you get."
~Zig Ziglar

"Words tell stories, and they also
reveal how we treat others with our
word choice."
~Trish Perry

I TEACH AN EIGHTH-GRADE HUMAN SEXUALITY COURSE at our church called Our Whole Lives.
I'll give that a minute to sink in.

Eighth graders, people—eighth graders! And human sexuality at church? We'll leave that for another story.

We were in class one morning, and I said the word "chest." No giggles, no eye rolls, no hitting each other. It was just another boring class.

But when I said the word "breast," it was like I was teaching a kindergarten class. The giggling started, the hitting of the arms, the eye-rolling. If you've ever met an eighth grader, you know what I mean.

Chest or breast. Very little difference except breast refers to a specific part of the chest. Men have them, women have them, so what is the big deal?

The big deal is that words matter. And words that you say to and about yourself matter.

In our initial sessions, my clients often say things like, "Yeah, I'm kind of good at that" or "I am sort of getting a promotion." Wow, two great things to say about yourself, and using the words "kind of" and "sort of" make them sound meek and unimportant.

This is called limiting language because you are not taking the full credit you deserve.

You can change those to powerful, forwarding phrases just by dropping "kind of" and "sort of": "I'm good at that" and "I am getting a promotion"; those words sound confident and powerful.

When talking about yourself, please do yourself a favor and *ban* the words "kind of," "sort of," and all other phrases like them. They diminish your true power.

Awareness is the first step to adopting forwarding language.

Journaling Challenges and Questions:

1. I have a challenge for you: over the next week, pay attention to when you use limiting language when talking to or about yourself.
2. How many times did you catch yourself? What were your limiting words or phrases?
3. How could you change the limiting words or phrases to forwarding language?
4. What difference does it make when you turn your limiting language into forwarding language?
5. Create a commitment around using forwarding language (e.g., "I commit to using forwarding language. I will partner with my spouse and coworker to point out my limiting language so I can change it to forwarding language").

#17
Mom Bangs

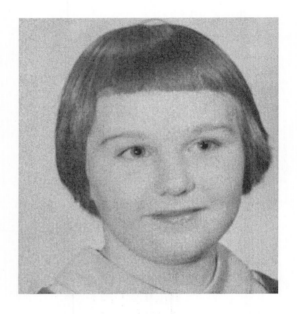

My sister Betsy sporting "Mom Bangs"

MOM: "PATRICIA ANN, LET'S CUT THOSE BANGS!" Southern mamas *always* use your middle name.

Me: "OK," I say with dread in my voice because I know what is coming.

Mom: "Have a seat right here." She sets up shop with Scotch tape and dull kitchen scissors.

Me: "Mom, not too short, *please*?" Why am I saying this? I know the outcome, but I have to ask.

Mom: "Hmm, let's see, that's about right." She takes a long piece of the Scotch tape and secures my bangs to my forehead. You see, Scotch tape makes a beautiful guide for a straight line. And she follows that line perfectly.

Me: "Mom, that hurts!" I complain as she pulls off the tape with a few hairs included.

Mom: "Oh, Patricia Ann!" Then she steps back to survey her work, realizing what has happened. "Oh my! We'll just do it one more time and fix this."

Me: "MOM!" And here starts "The Dance of the Scotch Tape": cutting, surveying, cutting, surveying, cutting, and finally, the words I *never* want to hear.

Mom: "Oh My! Well, they'll grow back."

My mom did this every month to all five of her kids. She never got the results she wanted, but this was how she was taught. It was a familiar path, and she just kept walking it, never getting to the end result she desired.

Does this sound familiar?

Not the bang cutting, but doing the same thing and expecting different results each time?

Why? Because doing it "that" way is familiar to us. We may have been told by our parents, teachers, and/or coaches that there is one right way to do it. Or, we have created a paradigm in our head that we can't do it any other way.

There are many reasons, but the result is the same: we end up where we did not want to go.

The big question is, "So, how do I change this?"

The answer is to take a different path, of course.

But that different path is unknown and not comfortable. It's not paved, so we will have to be more prepared to take that path.

This is best explained with a visual (at the end of this story.)

Both of the paths are in the woods, surrounded by trees and brush.

Both will take you to a destination.

Path A has been walked 1000+ times by you, so it has been paved. It is your habitual path. And this path is *not* going to take you where you want to go.

The other, path B, is rough. It's not completely clear and definitely not paved.

It will take you where you want to go and will likely be uncomfortable.

Path B is your Power Path! This is a different path than you have taken in the past.

It is uncomfortable, and you can't clearly see the path ahead of you, but you have a gut feeling it will take you where you want to be.

In fact, when walking your new Power Path, it is best if you wear boots. It's also important to bring a backpack of tools like a knife, a saw, bug repellant, bear spray, etc.

Of course, this is metaphorical. The paths I'm referencing are the neuropathways that are in your brain. The more you do something, the thicker those paths get, thus the paved path analogy. If you stop doing something habitually, those neuro pathways start to shrink.

This is a *very* simplistic explanation of how habits are formed.

The backpack? Those are all of the tools you learn through training reading, videos, therapy, coaching, etc. Tools like your inner critic and inner champion.

So, which path will you choose?

You get to choose your path, *you* get to choose where you are going, and *you* get to choose if you want to take the chance of taking a different path.

You get to quiet the voices inside your head that say, "This isn't the way you were taught." That voice is your inner critic, and it wants you to take the paved path to keep you safe and small.

The other path you can choose to take is your Power Path. Your inner critic does not want you traveling on this path because it is riskier and you might grow out of your old familiar habits. That is when the inner critic loses power.

The Power Path is *your* path. It is not anyone else's. You create it, you walk it, and you make it your new habit.

Journaling Questions and Challenge:

1. What do you currently do that is habitual and never gets you where you want to go? (e.g., Eating sugar, "winging" your day without planning, reacting vs. responding?)

2. What could you do to change just one of those habits? Take it slowly, changing one or a few habits at a time. You don't want to change 12 things at once because it is less likely that all 12 will become new habits. It is also important to create a cue for these habits, such as putting your workout gear next to your bed, so you immediately change into the gear to work out when you wake up. That becomes your cue to work out.

3. Write down 1-3 new habits you'd like. Now, for a week, read these habits every morning. In the evening, journal about them. What cues did you create for each habit? Were you able to stick to the habits? If not, what caused you to go back on your habitual path? If you did stick to your new habits, how did it feel? Keep this up for at least a week. If you like the results, continue this practice for four weeks and then consider adding 1-3 new habits.

VISUAL OF THE POWER PATH

Path A, Your Habitual Path

Path B, Your Power Path

Your choice

#18
Resilient in
Neon Pink

Hannah at 22 months in a Spica cast

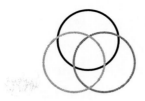

WATCHING MY 22-MONTH-OLD AND 4-YEAR-OLD playing on the small playset in the backyard was bliss. It was a spring Sunday, 70 degrees and sunny. We would relax the whole day.

And then the fall: "Mama, Mama, Hannah's hurt!" She'd fallen off the playset, and we had to take her to the emergency room immediately.

It was like a whirlwind; one minute we were trying to soothe her and the next minute we were waiting for her to come out of a two-hour surgery for a spiral fracture of her femur.

In the recovery room, I was invited to get into her bed to comfort her when she woke. They pulled back the covers and…what? There was my baby with a Spica cast up to her chest and down to her toes. And it was neon pink!

She woke and pulled at her IV. The nurse took it out.

She hit her cast and said, "Off Mama."

"Sweetie, that's like a Band-aid on your body to make you better. You have to keep it on."

She never complained again.

It took all of one day for her to adjust to this contraption, holding her body stiff.

She lay on her stomach and army-crawled or rolled to get from place to place. She was happy playing with her brother, the dog, and her toys. She even figured out how to throw the basketball into the hoop from the wagon.

In the six weeks she had the cast, Hannah never complained once, even though her life had been completely changed.

She was the epitome of resilience in neon pink!

When adversities happen in your life, how do you react or respond?

Are you like Hannah, accepting adversity and figuring out how to deal with it in a positive way? Or do you turn to anger, denial, tears, or depression as many of us do?

Children are naturally resilient. Adults? Most, not so much!

So, how do you become more resilient? How do you build that muscle that seems to be nonexistent in hard times?

Some tools to help are, 1) intentionally capturing three things you are grateful for each day, 2) meditation (there are many guided meditation apps and videos), 3) deep breathing, 4) journaling, 5) self-care, 6) learned optimism (yes, you can learn to be optimistic), 7) laughter, and more. Googling "how to be resilient" will give you more tools.

I became a coach because of the adversity I experienced, including the loss of loved ones, sexual abuse and rape, a layoff, breast cancer, and many others.

Initially, my resiliency muscle was weak, but I built it up over time. I tried different tools, testing what worked and what didn't. I am still adding tools because a hammer doesn't help when you need a screwdriver!

Now, as a coach, I help people to build that resilience and find their power. I love my vocation.

You *can* build resilience in your life.

Journaling Questions:

1. On a scale of 1 to 5, where would you rate yourself in resiliency?

   > 1= I have no resiliency. Anything negative affects me to my core and it takes me a long time to work through it. 5= Resilency is my Superpower. I have the tools and skills to work through any adversity in a healthy way.

2. What are some of the tools you know that can help with adversity?

3. What tools have you tried, and what caused them to work or not work? Note: Every adversity is different. You may need different tools for different adversities.

4. What tool/s are you willing to try in your next adversity?

CONSIDERATIONS ON RESILIENCE...

"A good half of the art of living is resilience."
~Alain de Botton

"We could never learn to be brave and patient, if there were only joy in the world...."
~Helen Keller

"Resilience is our ability to bounce back from life's challenges and unforeseen difficulties, providing mental protection from emotional and mental disorders."
~Michael Rutter

#19
SHOTGUN!

"SHOTGUN" TRIVIA

Why do we call "shotgun" to sit in the front passenger seat?

Calling "Shotgun!" before anyone else getting in the vehicle assures you get the front seat next to the driver. You get extra legroom, control of the radio, help navigating, and personal pride.

But why say "shotgun?" Why not just "front seat"?

In the old west, carriage drivers brought along someone to sit next to them to protect them and their valuables, usually carrying a shotgun. In the classic John Wayne movie *Stagecoach*, co-star George Bancroft proclaims, "I'm going to Lordsburg with Buck. I'm gonna ride shotgun."

WE WOULD BE LEAVING to go to the store with Mom and someone would yell, "Shotgun."

Darn, that meant they got to ride in the front seat with mom. That was *my* favorite place.

I had four older siblings and they knew more than I did, like when to call "Shotgun."

I learned quickly that the first to yell shotgun laid claim to the coveted passenger's seat.

I soon figured out that if I would go to my mom and whisper, "Shotgun," no one would hear and Mom would back me up that I said it first.

I had to find creative ways to survive as the youngest of five kids. To me, riding shotgun was one way I survived because, in the back seat, my siblings would get on my nerves, saying things like, "Mom, she's looking at me!"

I loved riding shotgun because:

1. I got to be closest to mom and have her attention
2. I had the best view
3. I had control of the radio station
4. I was important because I helped navigate. My mom would say, "I've got to keep my eyes on the

road, let me know when you see the Jewel (our local grocery store.)"

And there was one caveat…you had to be positive and helpful, otherwise you were replaced with another sibling who would fulfill that role.

Who rides shotgun with you? Not in your car, but in your life? Who helps you navigate?

Is it your inner critic (see story 11) or your inner champion?

Your inner critic is that voice that tells you negative messages and keeps you "safe" or stuck. Think about a time that you talked yourself out of doing something because you didn't think you were good enough or as good as someone else. That it was your inner critic.

Your inner champion is the voice that is your motivator and tells you, "Yes, you can do this!" Think of a time when a great thing happened to you. That is your inner champion voice.

Believe me, my inner critic was in the passenger's seat for over 25 years of my life, trying to keep me safe and small. There are a lot of things I wish I would have done or situations that could have been so much better if my inner champion had been there. But the past is the past, and I can learn from it and let my inner champion ride shotgun now!

My wish for you is that you put your inner critic in the back seat and let your inner champion help navigate your life.

You deserve it!

Journaling Exercise and Questions:

1. Sit in a quiet space with two blank pieces of paper.
2. Close your eyes and think about a situation where you talked yourself out of something you really wanted to do or a time when you doubted yourself.
   a. What are the messages you heard in your head?
   b. Write them down; this is your inner critic.
   c. What do they look like? Give them an image and a name.
3. Now, think about a time when something great happened in your life.
   a. What are the messages you heard in your head?
   b. Write them down; this is your inner champion.
   c. What do they look like? Give them an image and a name.
4. Who navigates with you the majority of the time in your life? Your inner critic or inner champion? Be honest; you're the one who knows the answer.
5. Pay attention to your inner critic this week and try to replace them with your inner champion. Journal how many times your inner critic demotivates

you. How many times were you able to call on your inner champion?

6. At the end of the week, answer these questions and write the answers in your journal:

   a. Who is really riding shotgun with you?

   b. Who is helping you navigate to a positive place vs. getting you lost?

   c. Who do you prefer, your inner critic or your inner champion?

#20

I'm Sorry,
What's Your Name?

MY FAMILY IN NORTH AND SOUTH CAROLINA usually have names that end in "ie", "y", or they have two names. Family names are Sissy, Bobby, Cindy, Ernie, Ricky, Jimmy, Donny, Letitia Jean, Johnny, etc.

I was given the name Patricia Ann Frank at birth. Down South, my mom called me Patricia Ann. I loved it, but only in the South! Otherwise, I hated the name Patricia. It just sounded ugly to me.

Truth be known, when growing up, I wanted to be "Heather." No, I never knew a Heather, but I thought Heather sounded so beautiful, almost ethereal!

I'd imagine going to school and my teachers calling, "Heather?" I'd proudly respond, "Yes Ma'am." All of the girls would ooh and ah because they'd think the name was so beautiful and they wished their names were Heather too!

Actually, I came by hating my name honestly. My Mom was born Gladys Lynn Quigley. She hated her name.

To be honest, that is quite a mouthful to saddle a baby with!

Luckily, they called her Sally Bet as a baby and Betty as a child. Betty is the name she always used. Betty is a nickname for Elizabeth. So, when Mom got married in the 1940s, she changed her last name *and* her first name. She became Elizabeth Quigley Frank—no more Gladys Lynn Quigley!

Think about that, it was the 1940s and she had the "audacity" to change her given first name. She told me some people in her hometown of Rocky Mount, North Carolina, found out and would say, "I'm sorry, what's your name?" and give her those disapproving looks we've all seen from a judgy neighbor.

I don't think she had the "audacity"; she had the "hutzpah"!

What's wrong with changing your name? What if the name you were given just doesn't fit you?

Society accepts coloring our hair, wearing makeup, wearing contacts, getting braces, changing where we live, and changing careers.

If it is ok to change all of those other things because we want to feel better about ourselves, is it really that different to change our names?

While I no longer want to change my name to Heather, there are other changes I might make if I could.

If I could wave a magic wand, I'd remove my extra chins. I think I have a turkey neck, and it'd be great if that extra skin was gone. Too bad I don't have an extra $15k hanging around for the surgery. Plus, I really don't want to have surgery. But who knows, maybe I'll win the lottery and rethink that.

The point is, that change is up to the person who wants it. They may not be comfortable, don't like what they have, or don't feel aligned. We all deserve to feel good about ourselves and our choices, whether the choice is about our body, our career, our beliefs, or even our name.

Journaling Questions:

1. What would you change if you could?
2. Is your change acceptable or unacceptable by society?
3. What would it take for you to make the change?
4. Are you willing to make this change? If so, when will you do it?

#21
No, STOP!

IT WAS 3:00 A.M. WE WERE LAUNCHING TARGET.COM with Amazon technology in four hours. I had been working almost 24 hours with no sleep. This was a huge project for Target.com that would change our business.

At 3:05, I received an email from "Sue" at Amazon with what she deemed good news and bad news. We would be launching on time, *but* the search tool would not be ready for launch.

"Really? This is one of the major reasons we chose Amazon as our tech partner. And you're telling me this four hours before launch? Unbelievable!"

With frustration, I forwarded the email to my boss, ranting about Amazon and that we wouldn't be launching with search. I used a few choice words and finished my email. I hit "send." At that moment, my heart stopped, and I yelled, "No! Stop!" I realized I had not forwarded the email but had actually hit reply. Now my heart was racing.

My ranting email would be in Sue's inbox within seconds. I dreaded the consequences. In fact, in 30 seconds, I had convinced myself that I would be fired, my husband would ask for a divorce, he would get custody of the kids, and I would be homeless, living in a van down by the river!

I was frozen. I could not even fathom what my next step would be, but I knew I was running out of time. Amazon would be calling my boss and I'd rather she heard the news from me than them.

I took a deep breath, printed the email and sprinted to my boss's office. She was sitting in her office with the VP and the president was also there.

Out of breath, I handed her the email. "I am so sorry. I was forwarding an email to you from Sue at Amazon saying we would not be launching with search. But I replied instead of sending it to you. Here is a copy of the email. It's not pretty."

She read the email and handed it to Cathy, the VP, who looked at me and started laughing! "Trish, it's not great that you sent that. But it's ridiculous that we would launch without search. I understand why you're so upset.

Thanks for letting us know *before* we got the call. Yes, we will definitely hear from Amazon and we will work through this. We've all made mistakes and this one goes in the record book." She smiled at me.

I breathed a sigh of relief and shared my plan to communicate this mistake to my team. I'd describe the failure to show them what not to do and have them brainstorm what I could have done. We'd problem-solve this together.

Cathy said, "Great idea, Trish. This is a great way to teach everyone *and* show your vulnerability. I'd actually like you to talk to our entire team." Vulnerability, or being more open, was on my development goals, but I didn't expect this!

And she was right. I created training for our entire team and got great feedback. The vulnerability of sharing my failure actually helped change the way I led my teams going forward.

Henry Ford was right, "Failure is the opportunity to begin again, this time more intelligently."

Journaling Questions and Tool:

1. What are some of your biggest failures or mistakes?
    a. How did you respond in these situations?
    b. Did you go into fight, flight, or freeze mode? What happened?
2. Now, look at the F.A.I.L.© model on the next page. I demonstrated this in my story, but without explicitly naming the F.A.I.L.© steps. Can you see how I employed the model?
3. Now, put the F.A.I.L.© method into action with one of your past mistakes or failures. Write down the steps and what you would have done differently had you known about this method.
4. How can you remind yourself to use the F.A.I.L.© model going forward?

F. A. I. L.© Tool

Here are four steps to take if you make a mistake or fail. I am going to ask you to F.A.I.L. © after you have failed. F.A.I.L. © is an acronym for steps you can take to lessen the impact of the failure and increase your learning.

F: Focus. Focus on what you did, why you made the decision, the outcome, and the consequences. Do *not* focus on the narrative you've created.

A: Acknowledge. Accept responsibility for the mistake. Do *not* blame!

I: Identify. Identify ideas or solutions to the problem. Identify your next steps. Communicate the mistake or failure and your solution to your boss, your client, team, peer, spouse, friend, etc.

L: Listen, Learn, and Lead. You will get feedback that will likely help you if you share your mistake or failure. Warning...be prepared; the person may yell at you or make you feel guilty. Don't react. You need to let the person internalize what has happened. You don't want to make a situation worse. Listen, take a deep breath, and respond calmly. What have you learned from your mistake or failure? How can you use the learnings to lead your team, coworkers, or others?

We all fail, 100% of us! And failing is what helps us learn. Failing is an integral part of learning and succeeing. Here's to all of our failures!

CONSIDERATIONS ON FAILURE...

"Only those who dare to fail greatly can ever achieve greatly."
~Robert F. Kennedy

"I haven't failed. I've just found 10,000 ways that won't work...."
~Thomas Edison

"You can't let your failures define you. You have to let your failures teach you."
~Barack Obama

#22

Oh, Gross!

What is a Lemon Cooler?
Think of a Nilla Wafer covered in lemony powdered sugar and you've got a Lemon Cooler. Sunshine Brands made this cookie in the 1970s

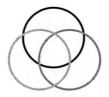

HAVE YOU EVER EATEN LEMON COOLER COOKIES? My brother *loved* these.

Sometimes he'd stick his hand in the bag yelling, "Oh gross!" His hand would emerge with sticky wafers, no powdered sugar. "Mo-ooom! Somebody licked off all the powdered sugar! Trisha!"

"Oh, don't be ridiculous, Daniel. Who in the world would do that? They're fine, just eat them."

Begrudgingly he'd eat one. When mom wasn't looking, he'd throw them away. This happened countless times. Who could the villain be?

Me!

My brother was seven years older than me. He tickled me until I peed my pants, called me Bucky Beaver (that's another story), and made fun of me.

The only control I had was my trick of licking powdered sugar off *every* cookie in the box. I'd laugh inside when he would get the box. "Gotcha!" I'd think to myself.

As kids, we often find passive-aggressive ways to deal with hurtful situations. Often, it's the only weapon we feel we have. Sometimes, this behavior spills over into our adult life, to our detriment.

When I was first married, I'd get mad when Jay didn't wash the dishes daily. The dishes would pile up. Instead of doing them myself, asking him, or suggesting we trade-off, I'd resentfully let the dish pile get even higher.

I got angrier every day as the pile became a small mountain.

After a few days, I couldn't take it anymore, and the dish situation ended in a horrible fight.

Jay explained that he had lived with roommates who washed dishes once or twice a week, and that was what he was used to. But, he was willing to change. He just didn't know it bothered me.

I also admitted to him that I had correlated his not doing dishes as a sign that he didn't really care about our marriage; I had completely made that up in my mind!

He hugged me and told me he loved me and always would.

Awful behavior over a pile of dishes that could've been averted with simple communication. Instead, I chose the passive-aggressive route. How did that turn out for me?

I'd feel guilty for days, having argued and assuming not doing the dishes meant he didn't care about our relationship. But his understanding and reassurance helped a lot.

Do I still create narratives in my head that catastrophize situations? Yes, but not as often. When I catch myself, I choose direct communication instead. It is so much more effective!

Journaling Questions:

1. What passive-aggressive behaviors have you displayed to your partner, kids, friends, or coworkers?
2. What was the outcome?
3. What are some ways that you can stop your passive-aggressive behaviors?
4. What commitment are you willing to make to curb your passive-aggressive behaviors?

#23

Oh No, Jan Brady!

'70s Friday Night TV Lineup ABC
   6:30 PM: Bewitched
   7:00 PM: Room 222
   7:30 PM: The Odd Couple
   8:00 PM: The Brady Bunch
   8:30 PM: The Partridge Family

I *NEVER* **MISSED THIS LINEUP OF SHOWS.** Friday night TV in the 1970s featured *Bewitched, Room 222, The Odd Couple,* **The Brady Bunch,** and *The Partridge Family*

The Brady Bunch was a defining part of my life, and I played right into the show's setup.

I yearned to be Marcia Brady, the oldest, with her long blond hair and "cool kid" vibe.

Cindy was the youngest Brady girl and played the "cute and sweet" vibe to its fullest.

And then there was Jan.

Jan was the awkward middle sister who never quite measured up to Marcia and could never be as cute as Cindy. No one wanted to be Jan. Jan had the "awkward" vibe.

I am the youngest of four girls and one boy in my family. At six years old, I compared the girls in my family to the Brady Bunch girls.

Vera is the oldest. She was the good girl and the homecoming queen. Truth be known, we all snuck a time or two wearing her tiara. She had the "cool" vibe of Marcia.

Betsy was the second oldest. She was the outgoing, gregarious one. She had a ton of friends and was so much fun. Betsy broke the mold of the Brady girls. She had the "humor" vibe.

Margaret was the sister closest to me in age. She was the sweet one. The one everyone liked. She was super smart and a very creative writer. My mom called her, "My sweet Margaret." She definitely took the "sweet" vibe of Cindy Brady.

Then there was me, the youngest. Shoot, all of the Brady girl roles were taken except one: the "awkward" vibe of Jan. My six-year-old brain decided that I was Jan Brady, the shy awkward kid who nobody really liked. Unfortunately, I took on this role and played it through high school, and into college.

I stayed in this role for at least 15 years until my first "adult" job at Goudchaux's/Maison Blanche in Baton Rouge, Louisiana. There were about 15 trainees who started together. None of us were from Baton Rouge, and all of us craved a great experience.

We all became fast friends. Baton Rouge offered me a rich social and work life that cracked open that shy and awkward shell of Jan Brady.

At work, I was promoted to the men's couture and designer buyer by 23. I traveled to Europe, attending designer shows, and to New York on buying trips. Definitely not what I imagined Jan Brady doing.

Socially, my friends and I discovered great restaurants, bars, and entertainment in Louisiana. I was in my element, and the "shy and awkward" vibe dimmed.

Did I say goodbye to Jan Brady? Externally, yes, but internally she hung around for a while. Little by little I became more outgoing and, dare I say, bold. I no longer needed Jan Brady to keep me safe.

My epiphany? I am not Jan, Marcia, or Cindy Brady. I have grown into myself and am so much happier!

Journaling Questions:

1. What roles do you play that really don't fit you? Maybe it was a role assigned during childhood, in your friend group, in your marriage, at work, or in other situations.
2. How does that role show up in your life?
3. What are the impacts on you?
4. Are you ready to shed that role and step into who you really are?
   a. If not, what will the consequences be of staying in that role?
   b. If so, what is one way you can start to shed that role?

CONSIDERATIONS ON YOU...

"When I was a child, my mother said to me, 'If you become a soldier, you'll be a general. If you become a monk, you'll be the pope.' Instead, I became a painter and wound up as Picasso."
~Pablo Picasso

"It doesn't matter who you've been. Now, it's about who you are willing to be...."
~Sheldon Ginsberg

#24

It's My Fault!

I OPENED THE MAIL THINKING IT WAS ANOTHER BILL. A $1,200 check from my insurance company? Bonus…until it wasn't.

I attempted to deposit my check only to find that my bank account was $2,400 overdrawn. What?

There was a $3,100 pending withdrawal from PayPal. Sometimes I buy things and forget I've used the money, but $3,100? I wouldn't forget that.

So, my bank account was shut down on a Friday. FRAUD!

This meant no debit card, no ATM, and no funds available until Monday. We were having two parties and I needed to go to the grocery store. What an inconvenience.

I would spend an hour at the bank reopening my accounts and at least another hour to reset my accounts to autopay my mortgage and others. What a pain, what a failure!

"I should have kept a better tab on my account."

"I should have protected my PIN better."

"I shouldn't have been so careless with my bank account and debit card."

"This was my fault!"

And then I heard my coach's voice, "Trish, what's a different lens on this issue? Is there another narrative or story?"

I often ask my clients to look through a different lens at their problems. Is there a different story I could tell myself? A different perspective?

Honestly, sometimes I like to stew in my own problems. For some reason, it feels good to feel bad, even resentful. Not today.

New lens? Well, I caught the fraud before the money was taken out of the account. Ok, I felt a little better.

I could use my Amex to buy my groceries and other things—I had options. I was beginning to come out of the resentment.

And, this was fraud, it wasn't my fault! Fraudsters find ways to steal, no matter what safeguards you put in place.

A foreign concept for me to accept that it wasn't my fault.

And let's face it, with everything else going on in the world like wildfires, hurricanes, flooding, Ukraine, and others, this was a drop in the bucket.

Ok, I emerged from my office knowing that I could handle this situation with relative ease. I had lifted myself out of the dark place and felt more in control, even proud of myself that I didn't let myself believe the narrative I was starting to create.

In the end, it wasn't my fault!

Journaling Questions and Challenge:

1. When was a time when you blamed yourself for something? Or a time when you made up a story about the outcome of something before you had the facts?

2. What was the narrative or story you made up?

3. What were the facts?

4. How could you have changed your lens and created a different narrative or story based on the facts?

5. Next time you blame yourself, write down the facts. Based on those facts, what is a different story or narrative you can create?

#25
More Mama, More!

Nicholas at 16 months with my mom

"CREEPY MOUSE, CREEPY MOUSE, CREEPY MOUSE, GONNA GETCHA, GETCHA, GETCHA!"

My mom crept her fingers slowly up my body until she got to my chin and then the tickling would ensue. "More Mama, more!" I would squeal.

Creepy Mouse, Gimme Some Suga', and Ride a Cockhorse to Banbury Cross were all childhood games my mom played with me. And I, in turn, played them with my children.

My kids would squeal, "More Mama, more!" And I would oblige, playing these games for hours. I not only reveled in their laughter, but I felt my mom beside me, egging me on and laughing with us.

Nicholas, my oldest, knew my mom for 18 months. She died at the hands of an incompetent surgeon. It was one of the hardest times of my life and I cried often.

This toddler didn't understand my tears of grief. I would cry and he would say, "Why Mama sad? Mama no cry, Mama laugh!" and he would mimic what I had played with him and start the Creepy Mouse game on me.

And for that moment, my grief would subside. I would laugh and squeal, "More Nicholas, more!" We were both happy and connected. And again, I felt my mom beside me.

Laughter and joy are to grief what a cooling aloe vera gel is to sunburn. The pain doesn't go away, but it subsides for a time. And in that moment, your life seems almost normal.

You still have to work through the entire path of grief and/or sadness, but laughter and joy lighten the load for you.

Personally, I have walked the adversity path many times with abuse, my mom dying, terrible bosses, being laid off, breast cancer, losing my sister to cancer, caring for my dad with dementia, his death, a severe concussion, and more.

I have come out on the other side stronger, more productive, and more joyful.

And in all of those adversities, there were times of joy and laughter, meditation, and being held up and supported by friends and family. During those times, my load was lightened and I would have renewed energy that allowed me to work through my grief.

Journaling Questions:

1. Are you experiencing grief now in your life? If so, how do you grieve?

2. If you are not experiencing grief now, think about times when you did experience grief. How did you grieve?

3. What supports do you have in place to help you with grief? Be specific. List the names of family members, friends, therapists or councilors, work resources, insurance resources, grief groups, religious support, books, websites, rituals, etc. Having these resources written in a list helps to find help when you are overwhelmed.

4. Where can you experience joy during grieving to lighten your load for a short period? For example, nature, outings with friends or family, a hobby such as art or cooking, exercise, YouTube videos of babies laughing (one of my favorites), funny TV shows or movies? Think outside of the box. Come up with a list and use it while grieving.

Note: many times we experience several losses at one time which cause grief. This is called complicated or cumulative grief. Processing multiple griefs together is hard and often takes more time. If you are experiencing this kind of grief or any grief that is overwhelming, it is helpful to seek out a professional to help process these griefs.

#26
Perspective From a Pink Station Wagon

A picture very similar to our Pink Wagon
growing up!
Courtesy of American Motors/Motor City Story of the Week

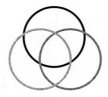

I MAGINE IT IS 1969.
A lovely light pink station wagon rests in the drive-way, being packed for our annual trek to the Caroli-nas. The Frank family (my maiden name) begins the yearly tradition of piling five kids into the pink wagon with a special feature of bars on the back window. A backseat prison, if you will.

My dad was an engineer, so we had homemade solu-tions to most things: the back prison bars, the luggage car-rier, and the back seat air conditioning.

He'd strap the homemade luggage carrier to the top of the car. Made of scrap plywood painted white, it resem-bled a simple coffin with an industrial hinging system and lock.

Mom would roll her eyes. "Oh Alvin, I declare!"

The best invention was the industrial tubes that ran from the front vents to the back prison, providing cool air. This was a necessity on a trip to the South. It was *hot*!

But there was hell to pay if you bumped the tubes and Dad had to fix them. "Why can't you damn kids be more careful" was heard many times.

In the back were blown-up pool mats for the kids' comfort.

We played car bingo and had coloring books, crayons, paper, and books to read.

And there was also a cooler with sandwiches, drinks, *lots* of fruit, and plenty of paper towels.

Too expensive to feed seven people at a restaurant, we'd stop at the gas station, fill up, and eat out of the cooler in the back of the station wagon. Our stomachs and bladders had to be connected to the gas gauge.

My dad didn't make more stops than necessary.

One of the stops he deemed necessary, besides a near-empty gas tank, was a shoddy road.

Dad worked for the Federal Highway Administration. He took his job *very* seriously, capturing every road issue on film.

Watching our home movies, you'll see the family smiling and having fun on vacation, then cut to a clip of a road, usually filled with potholes; then vacation scenes again. Unique home movies, indeed!

We were quite a sight in that light pink station wagon.

My siblings describe our vacations in similar ways, but with different details. There is a 13-year spread between the youngest and the oldest, and we each have a different perspective on our vacations.

For example, my oldest sister remembers the station wagon as coral. I remember it as pink.

My dad took copious amounts of photos. My oldest sister *hated* having her picture taken. I *loved* it and wanted more.

We were in the same family, same car, and on the same vacation. Yet memories and perspectives were very different at those ages. When we recall those vacations, we tease each other, knowing *our* version is the right one. It usually ends up in uproarious laughter.

But different perspectives can cause a lot of conflicts and can end friendships, marriages, and worse.

Our brains process information based on our prior experiences, memories, values, and other factors. No wonder we have different perspectives.

I often hear stories about conflicting stories from clients. I use those stories as a tool in to reveal the differing perspectives.

I have them tell their version of a story — their perspective.

I then ask them for the facts. Based on the facts and what others might think, they make up two other versions of the story that could be true. It becomes clear that others might have different perspectives.

Asking questions about others' perspectives and discussing the differences often leads to finding the common ground or understanding. The other person feels heard, and this helps to calm the conflict.

Journaling Questions:

1. Think about a time when you had a different perception about a situation than someone else that ended in an argument or other negative consequences.
2. What issues or differences were there?
3. How did the situation end?
4. What would have been different if you had asked clarifying questions about their perspective like, "What makes you think that?" or "How do you want this to be resolved?"

CONSIDERATIONS ON PERCEPTION...

"There are no facts, only interpretations."
~Friedrich Nietzsche

"What we see depends mainly on what we look for."
~John Lubbock

#27
Quitters vs. Survivors?

"There is a thin line that separates laughter and pain, comedy and tragedy, humor and hurt...."
~Erma Bombeck

T

"HERE ARE QUITTERS AND THERE ARE SURVIVORS."
I was dumbstruck and responded, "I'm sorry, what do you mean by that?"

"I said there are quitters and there are survivors. People who commit suicide are quitters."

His comment triggered my grief and sent me into fight, flight or freeze. I knew I couldn't react or I would say something coming from my emotional brain, not my logical brain. That would give him further reason to continue spouting his beliefs about suicide and I didn't want to give him that chance.

I closed my eyes and took a few deep breaths. I responded, "Sir, first of all, the accepted term is 'died by suicide,' and second, I will not discuss this with you. I have a very strong boundary about suicide. People die by suicide for many reasons, but they are not quitters. I will not discuss this any further."

I walked away. I stood up for myself and my beliefs, *and* I stood up for all who have been impacted by suicide.

My grief settled and I was proud of my response. I was able to continue my day in a productive way.

I thought about how this would have gone ten years ago and shuddered.

Ten years ago, I would have reacted. I would have been in fight mode and would have given this man a piece of my mind. I likely would have used a few choice words and the argument would have escalated.

This year is the 10th anniversary of my diagnosis of breast cancer. I often say cancer saved my life, which sounds strange to some people.

Breast cancer and all of the traumas that followed made me take a step back and look at how I was living my life. I quit my corporate job, and I became a coach instead of continuing my route as a "Corporate Badass Mom," as my son called me.

I have learned to pick my battles. I have learned to take deep breaths to bring my thinking brain, my prefrontal cortex, online. And I have learned to ask clarifying questions and to walk away when there's no sense in continuing a conversation.

I have learned to create and use boundaries for my well-being.

I have created boundaries around things that I am passionate about; my time, my work, my family, and my volunteerism. I have created boundaries around my life.

And it has made a huge difference. I am calmer, I am happier, and my son now calls me a 'Zen Mom.'

Journaling Questions:

1. How would you rate yourself in setting boundaries? 1 = I don't set them at all, 5 = I use boundaries all of the time.
2. If you are between a 1-3, what prevents you from setting and using strong boundaries? As an example, I am a recovering people pleaser and didn't want to have anyone not like me because I had boundaries.
3. In which parts of your life do your find boundaries most helpful?
4. If you don't set boundaries, in which parts of your life would boundaries be most helpful?
5. What is one boundary you will set today? How will you enforce that boundary?

#28
"I Will *Not* Be Held Hostage"

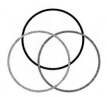

ISAT DOWN AND EXPLAINED TO MY EXECUTIVE VICE PRESIDENT, "John, from my team, was offered another job and would like to stay here. He has asked if there is anything we can do. I think—" My boss cut me off and slammed his fists on the table. "I will *not* be held hostage! Who in the hell does he think he is?"

"I don't think he's trying to—" was met with, "You don't think he's trying to what? Hold us hostage? Of course he is. He knows he has two of the most important projects on your team. Damn it!"

I just stared at him in disbelief. Then he dropped the hammer.

"Tell him we'll meet their offer, but in bonus form. Then, fire him in December before we have to pay him. I won't be held hostage!"

I sat there with my mouth agape. Integrity is one of my top values, and this situation had *no* integrity at all. At that moment, I realized my boss had no integrity either.

I tried to be calm and said, "I don't lead like that and I won't do that to him. If that's what you want to do, then you'll have to do it yourself. You know I'm going out on medical leave in a week, so I'll leave it to you. And I will not fire him in December if he accepts your offer. I'll leave that to you as well."

He just rolled his eyes; I was shooed away and he said that he'd handle it. What a prince!

Back in my office, I told John to think long and hard about the offer from my boss. He understood and he resigned the day of the counteroffer from my boss.

I would have resigned with him, but I was having surgery and needed time to think about my ultimate decision. I left the company seven months later. My boss made it easy for me to quit!

That was the day I realized that there was a huge difference between a boss and a leader.

A boss does what the word implies: bosses their team around. A boss has to control the outcome. They don't trust their team members to do the right thing. In my experience, bosses lose integrity every time they don't trust their team and tell them what to do.

A leader shares their vision with their team. They know their team members make them successful. They encourage, train, and motivate vs. "bossing" their team. Every *leader* I've had has had high integrity.

In my career, I've had a split: six bosses and six leaders. When working with leaders, I was the most productive and happy. Working for bosses, I was unmoti-vated and stagnant.

In my coaching, I specifically ask my clients how they like to be managed and if they'd rather work for a boss or a leader. We then discuss the behaviors that make them different.

The next step is for them to discern which style they are, a leader or a boss based on the behaviors they have listed. It is very enlightening to my clients. Every one of them wants to work for a leader and some realize they are actually behaving like a boss.

It is much easier to put a plan together to become a leader when you have a clear picture of how *you* want to be led and how you are currently behaving—as a boss or a leader.

Journaling Questions:

1. Think about bosses you've had vs. leaders. Who did you prefer to work with?
2. What behaviors did you like and dislike from each?
3. Ask yourself, "Am I a leader or am I a boss?" Even if you don't work outside the home, which are you?
4. What behaviors do you have that make you a leader? Are there any behaviors you would like to change?
5. What is one step you could take to become a leader, even if you are not leading a team?

CONSIDERATIONS ON LEADERSHIP...

"If your actions inspire others to dream more, learn more, do more and become more, you are a leader...."
~John Quincy Adams

"The key to successful leadership is influence, not authority."
~Ken Blanchard

"No man will make a great leader who wants to do it all himself or get all the credit for doing it...."
~Andrew Carnegie

#29

Does Grief Have a Shelf Life?

BACK FROM A DOUBLE MASTECTOMY, I was greeted with this comment, "It must have been nice to have six weeks off to do nothing but watch TV and read books."

And then there was this comment: "What's wrong with you? You don't seem like yourself."

Hmmm, I'd been diagnosed with and had surgery for breast cancer. I now lived in fear of my cancer metastasizing, possibly dying, and having to leave my family without a mother and wife. My body had completely changed: no breasts. The cancer medication affected my brain. My hormones were all over the board. Gee, why was I not myself?

I was grieving and living with a fear of the unknown! No, I was not myself…at least not my old self prior to breast cancer.

My best friend's grief is different from mine. Her daughter died by suicide. I can't even imagine that grief.

I was shocked when she told me what her boss said to her three months after losing her daughter. My friend was told that it had been three months and she needed to stop talking about her loss at work. She wasn't even talking about her loss—it was her coworkers who were concerned about her that were discussing it.

I was so pissed off! All of those comments were like saying grief has a shelf life, a timetable. IT DOESN'T!

At the end of the day, most managers and organizations don't like the really uncomfortable "people stuff" of grief. Grief is not something we like to talk about or deal with at home, let alone at work.

Grief has no prescribed process and there is *no* shelf life. Depending on the grief and the person, it could last five months, five years, or more.

Grief *is* uncomfortable "people stuff" and 100% of people will experience it in their lifetimes.

What causes grief? Often, losses cause grief, but there are additional reasons, a medical diagnosis, a mental diagnosis, a major career change, PTSD, an abusive boss or coworker, an abusive spouse or parent, a traumatic incident, a miscarriage, and the list goes on.

And grief is different for everyone. Some people hide it and don't want to deal with it. Some can't function "normally" for a time. Some have ups and downs. Some process grief verbally. Some become workaholics. There is no prescribed grief process.

Have you ever heard the phrase "separate your home and work life?" I will argue that it is hard to truly separate the two at any time...your work affects your home and your home affects your work. But with grief, it is even harder; grief is *going* to affect both home and work. Grief is a part of life; it is nearly impossible to compartmentalize it.

So, what do we do about grieving while in the workplace? Employees can't just quit their jobs, and they need to process their grief on their timeline for their well-being.

Some organizations think they have this covered with the 1-800 Employee Assistance Program (EAP). They don't. Grief is more personal than that. EAP is absolutely a resource, but not a wholesale answer. Also, the EAP doesn't help managers or coworkers learn how to work with the griever.

My idea? Provide coaching to grieving employees for support, helping them find their way back to engagement and productivity. Beyond coaching the griever, provide coaching to the manager *and* coworkers. In short, provide grief training to *everyone* in the company. People need to understand that grief is complex, it does *not* have a shelf life, and it lasts longer than expected.

What is a simple thing you can do? If a coworker is grieving, say something like, "I am sorry for all that you've gone through, I am glad you're back." Let them grieve and check in on them periodically to see how they are doing. Do *not* ask them what is wrong, when they are going to get over it, or when are they going to be themselves again. In short, be *kind*.

You see, there is also no shelf life for kindness; please be patient and kind with those who are grieving. We will all have grief in our lives.

Journaling Questions:

1. What is your experience with working and grieving?
2. If you were working while grieving, what was your experience with your supervisor and your coworkers?
3. How do you wish your experience would have been different?
4. What will you do differently to be kind to someone who is grieving?

CONSIDERATIONS ON GRIEF...

"Grief is itself a medicine."
~William Cowper

"Remember, the burden of sorrow is doubled when it is borne alone."
~Goran Persson

"The only cure for grief is to grieve."
~Earl Grollman

#30
If You Were
A Tree...

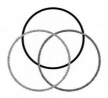

"IF YOU WERE A TREE, WHICH WOULD YOU BE?"
my coaching instructor asked.

I rolled my eyes. *What a stupid question*, I thought. I could be doing a lot of other things instead of this!

I finally acquiesced and actually put a lot of thought into this question.

A weeping willow! A weeping willow is the most compassionate and loving tree, in my opinion. It is accessible to and welcomes all. Its hardy trunk breaks into huge branches lower to the ground so children of all ages can climb it.

Its limbs reach down to let anybody, alter-abled or not, touch its soft leaves. It provides tremendous shade from the hot sun to all who seek it.

It is also playful, dancing with the wind, moving and rustling as if singing to music, and providing entertainment to all who want to partake.

Yes, I am a weeping willow!

I was with a client working on her values. After the exercise she completed she was amazed at the results. She had prioritized her top values.

"I'll admit, Trish, I thought this was a pointless exercise. Everyone *knows* their values and can prioritize them. Then I did your exercise and I understood the importance."

"My top six values were different from what I projected. I thought about your phrase of these being my core values. I imagined a tree. My six top values are the roots: they keep me grounded. The other parts of the tree—the trunk, branches, and leaves—are the other values that are also important to me. But my roots, my roots are what keep me grounded!"

Wow, this analogy brought all of the pieces together for me.

My top six values—love, well-being, family, integrity, friends, and compassion—are the roots of *my* tree. They keep me grounded. The rest, like giving, creativity, learning, gratitude, etc., are the other parts of the tree—of me!

With my client's permission, I now use this analogy in my business. It clearly resonates with my clients. Our root values keep us grounded, like a tree. What a wonderful image!

Journaling Activity and Questions:

1. Take some time to think about your values and list them on a piece of paper. I have included a list for your reference.

2. YOU get to define your values, not the dictionary. For example, you may include physical, emotional, and spiritual health in the word "well-being," or for you, "well-being" may only be physical health.

3. Which of these values from the list on the next page are the MOST important to you? Choose 5-7. These are your root values. Your root values help you determine why you might now agree with a situation and help you make decisions.

4. How will you use your values?

5. Just for fun, if you were a tree, what kind would you be? What are the reasons you chose that tree?

Core Personal Values

Authenticity	Creativity	Generosity
Achievement	Curiosity	Goodness
Adventure	Discernment	Grace
Artistic	Determination	Gratitude
Authority	Danger	Growth
Autonomy	Devotion	Happiness
Acceptance	Detachment	Harmony
Assertiveness	Design	Healing
Balance	Discovery	Honesty
Beauty	Dreaming	Hope
Boldness	Educate	Humor
Calm	Endurance	Humility
Career	Empathy	Inner Harmony
Coaching	Enthusiasm	Imagination
Compassion	Encouragement	Impact
Challenge	Exploration	Influence
Consistency	Fairness	Innovation
Collaboration	Faith	Inspire
Confidence	Fame	Integrity
Community	Friendships	Intellect
Competency	Fun	Joy
Contribution	Family	Justice

Core Personal Values (Cont'd)

Kindness

Knowledge

Laughter

Leadership

Learning

Love

Loyalty

Mastery

Meaningful Work

Mercy

Modesty

Nature

Nurture

Notoriety

Obedience

Openness

Optimism

Order

Peace

Planning

Pleasure

Popularity

Power

Practicality

Presence

Pride

Prosperity

Purposefulness

Recognition

Relationships

Reliability

Religion

Reputation

Resilience

Respect

Responsibility

Reverence

Sacrifice

Security

Self-Acceptance

Self-Discipline

Self-Love

Self-Reliance

Self-Respect

Service

Spirituality

Stability

Strength

Status

Success

Support

Trustworthy

Traditions

Tenacity

Tranquility

Teaching

Truthfulness

Unity

Understanding

Vision

Victory

Wealth

Wisdom

Warrior

Well-Being

Wholeness

CONSIDERATIONS ON VALUES...

"The decisions you make are a choice of values that reflect your life in every way."
~Alice Waters

A highly developed values system is like a compass. It serves as a guide to point you in the right direction when you are lost."
~ Idowu Koyenikan

#31

I'll Be Happy When...

I have a new car

I have a house

I have a bigger house

I am married

I have two kids

I get that promotion

I get a new job

I lose 20 pounds

I run a marathon

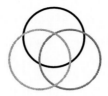

PETER SET A GOAL TO HAPPILY RETIRE WHEN HE HAD $10M SAVED.

He received a buyout offer for his company of $125M. Happy retirement, right? Well, yes, but a friend was offered $330M for his company, so Peter held out for more money.

One short year later, with no buyout offers, he experienced a complete devaluation of his company and went bankrupt.

Peter had renegotiated his "when." Now he had no money and his new "when" became "when I get out of debt" instead of enjoying retirement with $125M.

After reading Peter's story, I developed the "When and Now" exercise to help myself and others become clear that our happiness, success, financial stability, etc., can't depend on our "when." "When" is aspirational. Aspirations are great until your happiness, success, contentment, etc., become dependent upon them.

Why? "When" can be a moving target.

A person will be happy when they lose 10 pounds; they aren't happy with the 10-pound loss and 10 pounds becomes 20 pounds, 20 becomes 30, and so on.

They'll be happy when they get the new job at their current company that they wanted. Yet they still aren't satisfied when they get it, so then happiness becomes getting a job at a new company.

They'll be successful when they get the BMW. They get it and don't feel successful; success now becomes getting a corner office.

You get the picture. This is often referred to as the "Hedonic Treadmill." The more you get, the more you want and you are never satisfied — you are unhappy and discontent.

This is not the way I want to live; if I'm honest, it *is* the way I lived in the past.

I had to realize the reasons I am happy now, the reasons I am successful now, and not wait until "when." I am so much happier and more content now without the Hedonic Treadmill!

Activity and Journaling Questions:

My "When and Now" exercise can help you to break through that discontent.

1. Fill in the blanks, "I'll be _____ when _____." Clients have filled the first blank with happy, successful, content, safe, financially stable, a great parent, etc. The second blank is tied to achievement, e.g., I'll be happy when I lose 10 pounds or I'll be successful when I make $200,000.

2. Now read your statement. How are you feeling about it? What would you change?

3. The next step is to take that word you used, "I'll be _____" and restate it to "I am _____ now because _____" For example, "I am happy now because 1) I have a husband who loves me, 2) I have three happy and healthy children, 3) I love my job, 4) I have friends who genuinely care about me, 5) I have a wonderful home."

4. Repeat this exercise for as many "when" statements as you have.

5. Do you see how you are happy, successful, content, safe, whatever your "when" word is *now*? Your goal is just that: a goal or an intention. Your happiness or success does not need to be dependent on it.

6. Keep these in a place that you review often.

#32

Katie an' Da Beas' vs. Bucky Beaver

Me at age 11- Bucked Teeth and All!

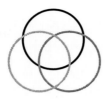

"AN' BESSIE, DON'T WATCH KATIE AND DA BEAS', IT BERRY CARRY!"

Translation for my two-year-old Hannah: "Aunt Betsy, don't watch *Beauty and The Beast*, it's very scary!"

As a family, this is one of the stories that we tell and laugh about over and over again. Hannah loves it and so does our family.

Versus:

"Remember Bucky Beaver? Trisha, you would get so mad when we called you that. It was so funny!"

This is said in jest, followed by a few chuckles from my siblings.

The difference between Hannah's "Katie and Da Beas" and my "Bucky Beaver" story is that I *hate* mine. Being called Bucky Beaver made me feel like I was an outcast as a child. It made me feel unloved.

My siblings were also kids at the time. Kids tease each other, sometimes in mean ways. I get it, and it didn't make it hurt any less.

I was about 11 years old and my teeth started to stick out. As you can see in the picture, my teeth were, in fact, buck. I feel so bad for that 11-year-old.

At 12, I got braces, my teeth straightened out, and I no longer carried the moniker of Bucky Beaver on the outside.

But inside, Bucky Beaver lived on for years. Inside, I didn't fit in. Inside, I was ugly. Inside, I was insecure.

Why was I holding onto this when it no longer served me? For me, Bucky Beaver let me stay a victim and gave me a "reason" I was not confident. It gave me an excuse to stay where I was vs. trying on confidence. Confidence was scary to me!

It took a lot of work, and the realization that this was a child's fear. This fear didn't have to follow me into adulthood. Holding onto this moniker no longer served me as an adult. I became more social—pushing out of my comfort zone, gathered evidence—compliments, practiced confidence and faked it for a long time. I finally shed my fear and became more self-confident.

P.S. One of my sisters gets my newsletter. After she read it, she called me and apologized. She had no idea how much pain "Bucky Beaver" had caused me. It was only by being vulnerable and sharing my story that she realized the impact and apologized. Of course, I accepted her apology and was very grateful to her for reaching out to me.

Journaling Questions:

1. Is there anything from your childhood that no longer serves you?
2. What is your Bucky Beaver story?
3. How is holding onto this story serving you? For me, it kept me as a victim and gave me a "reason" I was not confident. It gave me an excuse to stay where I was vs. trying on confidence. Confidence was scary!
4. What do you need to move past this story? I had to write my story down, and write all of the feelings I felt as a 10- and 11-year-old child. Finally, I wrote a letter to my 11-year-old, so she finally felt understood. As an adult, I had resented her all of these years because she was holding me back from being confident. It wasn't her fault.
5. What is one small step you can take to shed this story in your life?

#33
The Deep End

"Sometimes the best results come when you are thrown in the deep end."
~Nathalie Cook

"Challenge yourself, jump off the deep end and learn to swim."
~Carson Kressley

"I DID IT MOM, I CAN SWIM IN THE DEEP END!"

I ran waving the black seahorse patch for her to see. I had passed my "strong swimmer" test at SkyLine Pool.

"I declare, Patricia Ann, you are a right good swimmer!" I loved her Southern mama accent.

She pinned on my patch and off I went into the deep end.

At seven years old, all of my friends had been swimming in the deep end since May; it was now July. I had failed the test twice.

But today I joined them and they cheered for me.

In the deep end, you had more choices. You could dive for "jewels" hidden at the bottom of the pool. You could just hang onto the wall and talk. You could jump off on the low dive and, more importantly, the high dive. The deep end was fun!

The deep-end kids had choices. They came to the shallow end when they wanted a change and then swim back to the deep end. I wanted that choice.

Now I got to spend the rest of my summer going between the deep and shallow ends. It was all I had imagined and more. More because I became a stronger swimmer, it gave me independence and choice, and it gave me immense confidence.

In life, we can choose where we swim, and we get to define what the deep end is.

For me, the deep end of life used to mean climbing the corporate ladder. I thought the more letters in front of, or behind your name, the better! Remember, I was a CBAM—Corporate Badass Mom

In hindsight, for me, that was a very narrow view of the deep end.

Now, living life in the deep end means living life to its fullest. It means lifelong learning, trying new things, enjoying simple things, and engaging deeply in conversations and relationships. Living life in the deep end means having choices. I can choose to hang out in the shallow end, the deep end, or in between.

One of my clients completed a six-month program with a 183% improvement in her goals. When I thought about why she had such stellar success, I coined her a "deep-end" client.

Why?

She came to coaching wanting to swim in the deep end, immediately. We would spend time in the shallow end, learning skills, and then venture into the deep end to strengthen and hone these new skills. She put her heart and soul into each session, and we created a Power Path for her. She was bound and determined to get every last benefit from coaching that she could…and she did!

She has now started her journey to get her Ph.D. She'll leave with a backpack full of gear, coaching skills and tools, to swim in the deep end of this new chapter of life. And she brings with her the choice of where she wants to swim.

Journaling Questions:

1. How do you live life? Safe, in the shallow end, or with the choice to cross into the deep end? Define the deep and shallow ends for yourself.
2. If you swim in both, what benefits and/or issues have you had in the deep and shallow ends.
3. How would you like to change your life to be safer or take more risks?
4. How can you do this?

CONSIDERATIONS ON LIVING LIFE...

"Twenty years from now you will be more disappointed by the things you didn't do than by the things you did."
~Mark Twain

"The purpose of life, after all, is to live it, to taste experience to the utmost, to reach out eagerly and without fear for newer and richer experience."
~Eleanor Roosevelt

#34

Passion vs. Image

Empowering rescued victims of human trafficking, sex and labor slavery with their God-given right to Life, Freedom, Education and Autonomy.

I AM BEYOND THRILLED AND HONORED.
I've been asked to sit on the board of advisors for the
You Are My Light—YAML Foundation & Trust.

Orly Amor started YAML in 2021, a nonprofit, non-governmental faith-based organization dedicated to empowering survivors of human trafficking, sex slavery, and labor slavery to reclaim their God-given right to life, freedom, education, and autonomy.

Did you know that there are over 25 million people that are victims of modern-day slavery and only 1% escape? And of that 1%, very few get a chance at life.

Because of this, Orly has set a mission to build regional healing centers in North America to provide rescued victims of human trafficking, sex slavery, and labor slavery with the resources to *Live Life Free.*

During my interview, I found they were looking for skills and experience, but more importantly, they were looking for a passion for the cause, a passion for the hard work, because it is a *working* board.

In reality, folks sometimes join boards to add to their résumés. Let's face it, it looks good to be on a board…it checks the volunteer and the leadership boxes, it creates a philanthropic image.

Initially, I was disheartened to think that someone would take a board spot to pad their résumé.

And then I asked myself, "What have I done to enhance my image that I wasn't passionate about?"

It's sobering to ask that question. How could I be disheartened with others when I, myself, had volunteered for things I wasn't passionate about to enhance my image?

Years ago, I was asked to join a board for a dance organization focusing on people with disabilities. My friends had children who were part of this program. I was very supportive *and* I didn't have a deep passion to join the board.

But I joined the board anyway. Why?

I was supportive of the organization and I felt like I *should* join. How would it look if I said no? Would my friends think I wasn't supportive of people with disabilities like their kids? Would I lose a friendship? If I joined, I wouldn't have to worry about that *and* it would look good on my resume…so I joined.

Two months into my term, I realized I was shortchanging this organization. They deserved someone who was passionate about their mission. They deserved someone who wanted to dig in to do the work. And I wasn't that person. I supported the organization monetarily, but it was not right for me to be on the board.

And guess what? I didn't lose my friends and they appreciated the honesty.

So, I am *thrilled* to join YAML, getting my hands dirty doing the work to provide rescued sex and labor slaves an opportunity to Live Life Free.

I get to live into my passion by living into my purpose and integrity vs. my image with this opportunity.

Journaling Questions:

These are NOT easy questions to answer, but they are enlightening.

1. Looking back, what have you done outside of your passion because of guilt, image, or another reason?
2. What would you do differently today?
3. How would your life be different if you did what you are passionate about?
4. What can you do to live into your passion now?

CONSIDERATIONS ON PASSION VS. IMAGE...

"One person with passion is better than forty people merely interested."
~E.M. Forester

"To be yourself in a world that is constantly trying to make you something else is the greatest accomplishment."
~Ralph Waldo Emerson

#35

True Leadership

A donation of _$50 (208 meals)_ was generously given in
your honor to send hope to hungry children around the world.
Each Feed My Starving Children MannaPack™ meal is lovingly
hand-packed by volunteers and provides essential nutrients a
starving child needs to gain strength and health.

Hi TRISH -
I NOTICED IN YOUR BIO
THAT YOU HAVE A CONNECTION
TO FMSC -
I HOPE WE CAN BLESS SOME
KIDS WITH A MEAL TOGETHER
BE WELL -

The donation card I received from a true leader!

I GAVE THE KEYNOTE PRESENTATION FOR A TEAM STRATEGY SESSION.

Failing Fearlessly for Success was the topic the client chose and is one I love to present.

I agreed to speak for free as it was for a client I *adore*! The keynote was added last minute and there was no money budgeted. Her leader, the director of the department, was grateful.

The meeting was wonderful. The team of engineers was highly engaged and several told their own stories of failure.

Frankly, I was surprised!

The fact that the leader of the team had agreed to have a keynote on failing for his group of engineers was my first clue that this guy was likely a good leader.

Then, his team members were willing to be vulnerable and tell stories about their failures. That was my second clue.

Finally, this leader joined in the conversation, talking about how innovation comes from being willing to try new things, fail, learn, and try again.

Great leader, right? But wait, there's more!

I received a personal check from this gentleman as payment, thanking me for a great engaging kickoff for the strategy session.

Then, a few days later, I received this donation in my name for Feed My Starving Children to supply 208 meals to children in need.

Did I cry? Yep, I'm a crier!

He had read my bio I sent with my initial proposal. He noticed that I volunteered for Feed My Starving Children and decided to donate in my name.

I am blown away by the thoughtfulness of this man!

Honestly, a $10,000 check from the organization for payment would not have meant as much to me as his personal check and the FMSC donation.

Maya Angelou said, *"I've learned that people will forget what you said, people will forget what you did, but people will never forget how you made them feel."*

I doubt I will forget what this leader did, but I will *never* forget how he made me feel: grateful, humbled, and comforted knowing there are such thoughtful people in the world!

I had proof he was a great leader from my perspective. What about his employees' perspective? I checked with my client who is his employee. She eagerly offered, "Yes, he is a true leader and I love working with him."

I count myself as one of the lucky ones who has experienced his true leadership!

Journaling Questions and Challenge:
1. Have you reported to or worked with a great leader?
2. What are your criteria for a great leader?
3. How are you a great leader?
4. How can you embody the other aspects you appreciate in a great leader?
5. Challenge: Choose one of your criteria to implement. When will you do this? How will you measure it? Who will you partner with for accountability to be sure you implement this criterion?

#36
Vanity or Reality?

"Awareness is like the sun.
When it shines on things,
they are transformed."
*~*Thich Nhat Hanh

I THOUGHT I WAS JUST BEING VAIN.
I visited a plastic surgeon to ask if my reconstructed breasts could be "fixed."

As you've read, I had a double mastectomy in 2012.

In January 2013, I had reconstructive surgery and I've *hated* my breasts ever since.

The doctor I saw, Dr. Migliori, was incredible. He validated there really were issues with my reconstruction and that I wasn't being vain.

He asked me, "How you feel and what you tell yourself when you look in the mirror?"

I sobbed…

"I hate the way I look. I think I must've done something to cause the cancer. I try to never look at myself unclothed. I don't understand how my husband is still attracted to me."

He gently put his hand on my shoulder. "My dear, *you* didn't do anything wrong. There are many reasons for breast cancer, especially when there is a family history like yours." He paused…

"You need to know that you're not alone. I see many patients with similar stories. You shouldn't be reliving your cancer experience every time you look in the mirror. I'm glad you came to me. We can fix this and you'll stop reliving your cancer at the sight of your breasts."

I took a deep breath, fighting back the tears.

"I want you to look in the mirror and smile with satisfaction and self-confidence, not cry with sadness and regret."

I couldn't believe his compassion and understanding. I wasn't alone.

In fact, I started to think about how my reaction is similar to many of my friends, family, and clients who've had adverse experiences in their lives.

So many of us are triggered by things we see, hear, smell, taste, or touch because it reminds us of that adverse experience.

In my case, awareness has been a *huge* healing tool. I still don't like what I see when I look in the mirror, but I don't berate myself and relive my breast cancer experience. Instead, I hear Dr. Migliori's words: "*You* didn't do anything wrong."

I haven't had my corrective surgery yet, but just the awareness of my trigger that made me feel "less than" has helped me to gain self-confidence and not go to that negative place.

This is not a light topic, but it is one that we need more awareness around.

What do I want others to consider from my experience?

- Don't accept the status quo. If you don't like something, journal it, challenge it, and if possible, change it.
- Be aware of what triggers you and talk about it, write about it, and cry about it, but don't push it away or just let it be. Awareness is a healing tool! Note, that this may require some deep work with your therapist.
- Ask, "What can I do with my awareness?" Can you make a change, get rid of the trigger, or work to desensitize yourself to that trigger?

Journaling Questions and Activity:

1. Where are you accepting the status quo in your life?
2. What awareness are you pushing away?
3. Journal about your acceptance and your awareness.
4. What are some things you could do to change the status quo?
5. What is one step you will take to make a change?

CONSIDERATIONS ON AWARENESS...

"As my awareness increases, my control over my own being increases."

~William Schutz

"Every moment is a fresh beginning."

~T.S. Eliot

"Awareness can be a healing tool. Your awareness allows you to make choices in what you want instead of the past controlling you."

~Trish Perry

#37
Planning Divorce before Marriage?

Jay and I on our honeymoon

"ARGH, I'M GOING TO BE LATE FOR WORK."

I ran with my bags flailing to the Delta Club. I had to take a shower and get ready for work. It was 7:30 a.m. Monday, I had just landed and had to get to work by eight for a meeting.

This happened at least once a month. I'd work a full day on Thursday and fly to Los Angeles on the red-eye. I'd rent a car on Friday morning to go directly to work with my vendors. I'd work all weekend on new designs for Limited Express.

Then back to Columbus, Ohio, on the Sunday night red-eye to my job as a buyer at Express. I did this for a full year. And I was tired!

On top of work, I was trying to plan a wedding. Jay and I became engaged in January, 1990.

Honestly, most of the planning was falling on Mom because I was traveling so much.

Jay even came to Ohio when I was in town to clean my apartment and do laundry—yes, I married an incredible man!

Then came the call from Target in March. What? Leave my job at Express? No way!

But...I looked around at the female leaders. They either had an unhappy marriage, were divorced, or were single.

When you traveled with your passport 24/7 to be called overseas at any time to rework your product line, there wasn't much time for a social life, let alone marriage.

Is this the life I really wanted? If so, I might as well plan my divorce before we got married. And kids? How was I going to manage my job, my husband, and my kids? My conclusion was that I wasn't going to be able to do this if I stayed at Express.

Ok, I'd rather not plan a divorce, I'd interview at Target and create boundaries between work and home.

I got the job at Target and moved to Minnesota in May. We got married in August and I created a few boundaries. The key word is *few*.

Jay and I celebrated our 32nd anniversary this year. And it is because of this man's patience that we are still married.

My desire to climb the corporate ladder was strong and my boundaries were weak. Although I had created some boundaries at Target, I had still worked *way* too much...like 70–80 hours a week too much!

But after my scare with breast cancer, I became an entrepreneur in 2015. This time around I set strict boundaries. I went from working 70-80 hours a week to 40-50, and I take days off and vacations now!

It is sometimes hard to set boundaries, but it is worth it, I promise.

Journaling Questions:
1. What boundaries have you set at work, at home, and between work and home?
2. Do you need to set firmer boundaries to live your life joyfully?
3. Do you know anyone who sets and lives with clear boundaries? Ask them how they do it.
4. What is one SMALL boundary you can set right now? How will you enforce it?

#38

Brutal Honesty

STOP MAKING EXCUSES!

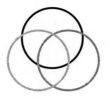

"BUT DAD, (INSERT EXCUSE AND WHINING)"
"STOP MAKING EXCUSES AND JUST GET IT DONE!"

I heard this at least once a week as a child and it hurt my feelings, every time. My feelings were easily hurt! As a kid, I thought my dad, The Colonel, was *mean*. In reality, he was brutally honest (and a little mean).

I had not thought about this for years, until my *awesome* business coach, Monica Shah, came along.

Monica is wickedly smart, funny, savvy, and friendly, and sometimes she is brutally honest (in a nicer way than my dad).

In fact, one day, she was teaching a group of 30 of us and I swear she zeroed in on me, just me, to deliver a message. I felt exposed. Once again, my feelings were hurt.

"The only one you're hurting is you... We are not in this game because we want to have excuses for why our business isn't working. We want our businesses to work... Don't allow yourself to hide behind excuses."

Obviously, she was speaking to the group, but it hit home so hard that I thought it was just for me.

The truth is, I was making excuses left and right for why my business wasn't where I wanted it to be.

Why? Because then I didn't have to take accountability. Then it wasn't my fault. Instead, I could blame it on the weather, the economy, the methodology, Covid, etc.

But at the end of the day, Monica was right, once again. I told you she is savvy!

You see, I was avoiding reaching out to people to talk about my business. I always had an excuse: "I don't want to bother them," "It's their busy time of the year," "I think I remember them saying they hated to be interrupted at work," and there were a thousand more excuses.

Monica's statement that if I wanted my business to work, I needed to stop hiding behind my excuses was right.

My butt was kicked into gear, my mindset changed, and my business doubled. *Thank you* for your brutal honesty, Monica Shah!

Journaling Questions and Activity:

1. What do you want to accomplish but haven't been able to?
2. Where are you making excuses that are actually holding you back?
3. Journal about your excuses
   a. Is there a fear that is causing you to make the excuse? Fear of failure, fear of success, imposter syndrome?
   b. What do you get from that excuse? Feeling like it isn't your fault, being off the "hook" to deliver? Feeling like you really shouldn't have to do the task?
   c. How are those excuses benefiting your goals?
4. What would make you let go of that fear to accomplish your goal?
5. What is one small step you could take to move forward to accomplish your goal?

#39

Unlikely Friends

V is for Vulnerability!

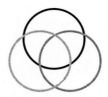

I WATCHED THESE TWO WOMEN AS THEY EASILY SLID INTO A CONVERSATION. They threw their heads back in laughter and teased each other with joyful banter.

To me, they were lifelong friends that fit so comfortably together and knew each other's secrets, deepest joys, and deepest sorrows. It was like watching a Hallmark movie and I wanted a starring role.

Instead, I felt like a third wheel.

Still, I don't know how, but I said, "You two are so much fun. I wish I had friends like you." And just like that, a lifelong friendship was formed. Robin and Melanie accepted me into their circle without hesitation or question.

Our friendship and bonds grew stronger as we met each other's spouses and friends and spent more time together. Soon there were six couples that hung out constantly. We shared birthdays, anniversaries, and holidays—our kids played together. We were sharing our lives and they changed my life for the better.

We call them framily because they are more than just friends, they *are* part of our family. These women are really my sisters. We are there for each other at every turn of life. And I am grateful every day that I chose vulnerability that day and asked them to be my friends.

Growing up, vulnerability was a four-letter word. Not the word you are thinking…it was the word *weak*.

So, at a young age, I put on my armor and never showed my vulnerability! Letting down my guard that day was one of the *strongest* things I've ever done and resulted in friendships that have stood the test of time.

The cool thing is that I never want to put on my full suit of armor again. Vulnerability has changed my life for the better, and I continue to test the boundaries.

Has anyone ever asked you what your Superpower is? What would you answer? Courage? Intellect? Kindness? Fortitude? Well, mine is what I used to consider a weakness; vulnerability!

My Superpower was uncovered the day I asked these women to be friends.

Vulnerability allows me to be myself, to share stories of my adversities that others often relate to, and to connect with people on a deeper level.

I hope you let your guard down sometimes and allow vulnerability to make you strong.

Journaling Questions and Activity:

1. What is your Superpower? Don't worry about being "too confident" in your answer.
   a. "I don't have one" is not an answer. Ask your friends, family, and coworkers…you have one, I promise!
   b. When you are at your best, people are drawn to you. What is that power?
   c. Some examples are Compassion, Influence, Negotiation, Communication, Organization, Strength, Resiliency, Grit, Questioning, Visionary, Financials, Translation (language or translating the complex into simplicity), Problem Solver, etc. Google this if you are not sure; you will find many others.
2. What does or would that Superpower allow you to do?
3. How would your life change if you fully embraced and used your Superpower?
4. Activity: Draw your Superpower symbol- it can be a badge, it can be a person, it can be whatever comes to mind.

#40
The Guest House

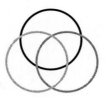

HOW MUCH ADVERSITY CAN ONE PERSON HANDLE? Imagine losing both of your parents within six months, being told you have to lay your team off, and knowing you will be next.

This was my client's world. She was not eating, not sleeping, and making bad decisions when I first met with her.

She was right. After her team layoff, she was told that she could either move to the company's headquarters or be laid off. We spent about a week talking about options, and then I introduced this poem by Rumi, "The Guest House."

We worked for several weeks uncovering what *she* wanted in life, and she chose the layoff. She moved to a different state, married her boyfriend, and found her dream job as a VP of Diversity and Inclusivity. Her life completely changed in three months because she looked at her situation through a different lens.

As in the poem, all of the "unexpected visitors" had come to her door and violently swept her house empty of furniture. And she had been cleared out for a new delight, of moving to a new city to marry her fiancé and land her dream job. She now had a life of power and joy. This joy helped her to work through her grief of losing her parents, and her resiliency grew strong.

She says that where she was once surviving, she is now thriving. I'm SO proud and happy for her!

The Guest House

This being human is a guest house.

Every morning a new arrival.

A joy, a depression, a meanness,

some momentary awareness comes

as an unexpected visitor.

Welcome and entertain them all!

Even if they are a crowd of sorrows,

who violently sweep your house

empty of its furniture,

still, treat each guest honorably.

He may be clearing you out

for some new delight.

The dark thought, the shame, the malice.

meet them at the door laughing and invite them in.

Be grateful for whatever comes.

because each has been sent

as a guide from beyond.

~Jalāl ad-Dīn Mohammad Rūmī (1207-1273)

Journaling Questions:

1. What are the most stressful adversities that have impacted your life?
2. After reading the poem, "The Guest House," what resonates with you?
3. What joy, depression, meanness, or momentary awareness can you welcome in and entertain?
4. How has this poem changed your 'lens' on life?

CONSIDERATIONS ON ADVERSITY...

"Every experience, no matter how bad it seems, holds within it a blessing of some kind. The goal is to find it."
~Gautama The Lord Buddha

"Every adversity, every failure, every heart-ache carries with it the seed of an equal or greater benefit."
~Napoleon Hill

"When you get to the end of your rope, tie a knot and hang on...."
~Franklin D. Roosevelt

#41
Hired at Eight Months Pregnant?!

Cathy David and me at my daughter Hannah's wedding in 2019

"CATHY, CAN WE SIT AND FINISH THE INTERVIEW?" I ASKED AS I GASPED FOR BREATH.

It was February 2000, and I was eight months pregnant.

Cathy David, my interviewer, was very high energy, conducted most of her one-on-ones and interviews while walking, and walked *very* fast.

I couldn't think and walk that fast, being eight months pregnant.

"Sure, I'm sorry. I should have thought about that. We can sit here."

We finished our interview and then walked back to Target more slowly.

"Jay, I got the job! I can't believe she hired me, I'm eight months pregnant!"

My husband just smiled.

Cathy David, the VP of merchandising, hired me to be the Sr. Group Manager for website operations at Target.com. I started on March 6, 2000, and was scheduled to have my baby, via C-section, on April 6, 2000.

What was she thinking? I would work for a month and then be out for 12 weeks. Really? She really hired me knowing this?

So, when I got back from maternity leave, I asked her that very question. Why had she hired me when I was eight months pregnant, knowing I'd be out for 12 weeks?

"Trish, I hire for talent and potential, not convenience. You hired a great team who made sure the work was done while you were gone. Now you are back and are going to make more great things happen. Why *wouldn't* I hire you?"

That comment is the essence of Cathy David.

Cathy David was not only my boss but is now a dear friend. She is a mentor and someone I look up to. She has integrity, a heart of gold, a high IQ, *and* an equally high EQ. She is an *amazing* woman, and I am blessed to have her in my life.

One of the saddest days in my career was when she left Target to spread her wings in other directions. But then and now she impacts my life in wonderful ways.

Now, when faced with a challenge, I often think, "What would Cathy David do?"

I am forever thankful that Cathy David is the person that I spent my working hours and even social hours with for a few years at Target.com.

I hope you all have a Cathy David in your lives that inspires you to be a better person every day.

Journaling Questions:

1. Who is your Cathy David?
2. In what ways has he/she/they changed your life?
3. When was the last time you told them how they impact your life?
4. Are you Cathy David to someone else?
5. How have you impacted their life?

#42
Facebook and Grief

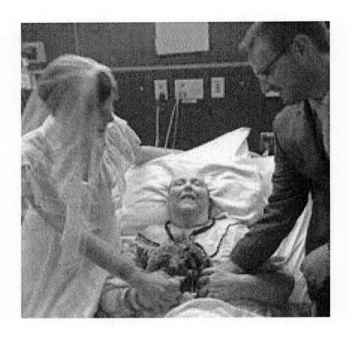

My sister Betsy with her son Danny and her daughter-in-law Mari

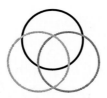

I STARED AT MY FACEBOOK MEMORY IN TEARS.

Normally there is a happy or casual memory, but not today. I was not prepared for this!

This is a picture of my sister Betsy, nine years ago. Her son and fiancé, Danny and Marisa, got married at her bedside in the hospital.

She died the next morning.

My sister had stage 4 malignant melanoma, and we had exactly eight weeks from her diagnosis to her death.

While this marriage at Betsy's bedside is a wonderful memory, it is wonderful when I want to remember it, not when Facebook reminds me. Not when I'm not prepared.

This is when I realized just how triggering Facebook memories can be.

One of my best friends lost her daughter to suicide on October 25, 2020. On top of that, she finalized her divorce in early 2022.

Facebook is a huge trigger for her as well. Pictures of her daughter pop up unexpectedly, triggering grief. And now pictures of her daughter and her ex-husband together create an extra layer of grief.

This triggering of grief is just the latest negative aspect of social media that I have experienced.

We both talked about just getting off Facebook. Who wants to be triggered in this way?

But then we agreed that with the pandemic, Facebook and other social media are a way of continuing connections that we are missing. Friends update about their family, friends, jobs, current events, etc. I like the connection!

The other day I got a call from a friend asking if I'd seen Julie's post from last week. I'd been off Facebook for a week… Julie's father had died unexpectedly from complications of Covid. I felt awful as I had not reached out to her or sent her a condolence message. I simply did not know. I wished I hadn't taken a break from Facebook or that one of my friends would have let me know. But there was an assumption that we all saw it on Facebook.

Facebook and social media are a double-edged sword providing both positive and negative experiences.

Yet, I continue to be drawn to Facebook. Yes, I am sure it has a lot to do with the algorithms that are designed to keep me coming back.

But honestly, it is the connection that keeps me coming back. I find comfort and familiarity in knowing Kris will post her Wordle stats daily, Vera posts pictures of her family on vacations and holidays, Dionne posts videos of herself dancing and inspiring others, Darrell updates the miracles of his cancer journey, Lauren and Cindy post pictures of Lauren's baby and the list goes on. I am connected to my friends and family on a daily basis.

For me, that connection offsets the negative trigger of grief on Facebook.

Journaling Questions:

1. What do you use social media for?
2. What negative experiences have you had with social media?
3. What positive experiences have you had with social media?
4. Based on your answers, does the positive outweigh the negative?
5. What boundaries can you put around social media?

#43

The Drunken Baby Walk!

Riley at 13 months demonstrating the Drunken Baby Walk

THERE IS NOTHING LIKE WITNESSING A BABY TAKING THEIR FIRST STEPS. Once babies crawl, they get a taste of independence.

Realizing they are mobile; they get curious and pull themselves up on any object. Then, they fall, but eventually they get their balance and stand.

Now the fun part, they realize they can take a step forward. But equilibrium is tough for a baby. They fall, get up and try again. And so it goes for the afternoon, day, week, or month.

Enter the drunken baby walk. Babies starting to walk look like they'll fall over anytime, and they do. At this point, adults applaud. Each time they fall, they are encouraged to get back up. They get up and do it again until they are running. Now they are totally mobile and parental containment is lost.

"I quit; this walking thing sucks!" said no baby *ever*! They pick themselves up and keep going. Every baby has a learning curve, and they don't compare themselves to their neighbor baby as we do as adults. Whether they are

10 months or 18 months, every able-bodied baby will eventually walk.

Most of us started out this way. We all crawled, stood, and walked. We all fell down and got up until we ran! When did our mindset change? When did we equate making errors to being a failure?

Friends asked Jay and me to play golf one weekend. "No, I'm sorry, I don't play golf."

They said, "It's ok, we will only play nine holes, and we aren't very good either." My husband said yes before I could decline again. Damn it, I didn't want to play. I didn't want to make a fool of myself. I didn't like doing things I wasn't good at.

I begrudgingly played nine holes. Yet, at about the second hole, I started to have fun. The four of us had a great time.

I shot a 98 that day, but truth be known, it was higher than that because my friends kept taking strokes off and calling those beginners mistakes. I'm sure it was more like 150 on nine holes.

But it didn't matter. I had fun, but I didn't really like the game itself. The fun came from the comradery and the laughter. I was glad I had tried something new. Giovanni Morashhuhi asked and answered, "Perfection? Being the most human you can be." And I was definitely putting aside my idea of perfection in playing golf that day. I was as human as I could be shooting a 150!

A lot of my clients are "closet perfectionists." They swear to me that they aren't perfectionists until we review their first assignment. The conversation usually goes something like this, "Just so you know, I didn't have a lot of time, so it is not my best work. I would have done a better job if I had time. Please don't judge me by this!"

To which I reply, "I'm thrilled that you did the work. Have you ever heard of a 'shitty first draft'? We will work on it together, and because you did the work, we have something to work from. And that's enough!"

I have a secret for you that took me 50 years to figure out...ready?...There is *no* such thing as perfection! Really, there is not. Just as beauty is in the eye of the beholder, so is perfection.

I encourage my clients and you to take that first step, write the shitty first draft, dance, be an artist, and do what you want without the fear of being judged, without the fear of not being perfect. Even when a virtuoso first picked up the violin, they weren't proficient. It takes time and patience, and we will likely suck the first time we try something. Brene Brown suggests that we "embrace the suck," and I couldn't agree more!

Journaling Questions:

1. Are you a perfectionist? No one is reading this, be honest with yourself.
2. If you are a perfectionist, even a little, what does this prevent you from doing in your life?
3. Have you enjoyed something but stopped because you weren't perfect or good enough?
4. What do you do exceptionally well? Were you as great as you are now when you first tried? How did you get so good?
5. Can you challenge yourself to do one thing that you enjoy but aren't good at? Before you decide on the challenge, first think about this question: "What is the worst thing that could happen?"

CONSIDERATIONS ON PERFECTION...

"I never expect to see a perfect work from an imperfect man."
~Alexander Hamilton

"Don't strive to be perfect, it is a lie. Perfection is in the eye of the beholder."
~Trish Perry

"They say that nobody is perfect. Then they tell you practice makes perfect. I wish they'd make up their minds."
~Winston Churchill

"Progress, not perfection...."
~Unknown

#44

Call The Coast Guard!

The cousins getting ready to board the pontoon boat

OUR PONTOON BOAT WAS CAUGHT IN A VIOLENT STORM ON THE EDISTO RIVER IN SOUTH CAROLINA.

Four-foot swells were crashing over the bow of the boat, and we wondered if this was the end.

So, we called the Coast Guard. The Coast Guard responded, "I'm sorry, we're busy, please call back." *What? We're about to die and you want us to call you back?*

Spoiler alert: obviously we didn't die.

Let me back up. We go to Edisto Beach in South Carolina every summer for a family reunion.

In 2005, our cousin installed a third pontoon on his boat to make it "ocean-worthy." Um, I don't think pontoons are meant to be in the ocean, but who am I to say?

He invited us for a boat ride. 16 of us went and we were excited about a relaxing trip down the river.

11 of us were dropped off on "Sea Shell Island" while the others continued their ride. We were supposed to be picked up in an hour. "Supposed to" are the operative words here.

We affectionately refer to the island as "Dead Horseshoe Crab Island." Why? There were dead horseshoe crabs everywhere, the bees were the size of small birds and it was over 100 degrees, all sun. Just imagine the stench! Oh, and those sea shells we were so excited to collect? There were live animals in all of them!

To top it off, we had no cell service.

Hell on earth is an understatement! Yet there we were, in Hell!

After three hours, our rescue boat pulled up. They lost an engine and were traveling at a speedy 10 miles per hour. We piled on the boat and headed back to the marina. We'd been rescued!

But this trip wasn't over yet; the tide turned and a storm was brewing. The trip home was even more miserable than our time on Dead Horseshoe Crab Island!

The wind and rain started. The canvas top on the boat acted as a sail and the wind picked us up and threw us around the river. Four-foot swells crashed over the boat.

We were soaked and the kids were scared. We sang songs, and told jokes and outrageous stories to keep the kids calm and happy.

Finally, fearing certain death, we called the Coast Guard, to no avail!

Would this nightmare ever end?

The boat finally slammed into a sand bar, where we waited out the storm.

It was not the relaxing trip we had planned!

Believe me, we never took a boat ride off the island again. Floating the waves on tubes and flying kites are now our idea of a relaxing vacation!

We now tell this story over and over again to everyone's delight. Someone always says, "remember that boat ride?" Everyone laughs and there is always a new detail that someone remembers. This story has become something that anchors (excuse the pun) us together. An awful situation has turned into fodder for connection and laughter.

Journaling Questions:

1. What's one story that was awful at the time it happened and you laugh about it now?
2. How did the situation go from awful to funny?
3. How do negative situations normally affect you?
4. How quickly do you bounce back from negative situations?
5. What methods do you use to recover from negative situations?
6. What could you do to practice being resilient?

#45
Reality TV and Chocolate

My attempt at chocolate decadence!

WHAT WORDS DO I USE TO DESCRIBE REALITY TV IN GENERAL? SNARKY, DRAMA, FAKE AND ABUSIVE ARE A START.

TV shows like *Housewives of...*(fill in the blank), *Keeping up with the Kardashians*, *Survivor*, *MasterChef* and others are set up in a win/lose situation and the drama is what pulls us in.

Some people who watch call it their guilty pleasure and I get it!

Why? Because sometimes it is nice to see someone with as much or more drama than we have. Sometimes it is like watching a movie and trying to look away at the scary parts, but being drawn in by the suspense. Sometimes it is an unbelievable story like *Tiger King* and its shock value is undeniable.

In my opinion, these shows exploit people for ratings. Do these people sign up for it? Absolutely. But I still don't like it!

Then I watched *School of Chocolate* on Netflix and it challenged what most reality TV has become.

School of Chocolate is a cooking school with a contest built-in.

The chef, Amaury Guichon, is a teacher, a mentor, a coach, and a cheerleader to *all* of the contestants, not just the winners. Each week he displays one of his amazing chocolate creations and then teaches them the methods he used to create his masterpiece.

The drama is about the creations, not about the in-fighting and backstabbing. And no one gets voted off the island. Someone does win, but *no one* loses! They all walk away with more skills and more knowledge.

The suspense is in watching how the contestants use the knowledge they learn from the chef to create master-pieces. They are bringing their mastery to the next level. Don't get me wrong, there is competition, but on a healthy level, not a toxic level.

The judging is about how well the person meets the challenge of the week *and* how they are participating and helping other team members succeed.

In fact, each week, Chef Amaury takes the bottom two contestants and works one-on-one with them to teach and enhance their skills so they can continue to play.

What words would I use for this show? Inspiring, hopeful, positive, entertaining, and supportive. These are a far cry from the words I started with. While watching the show, my mindset became more positive.

I talk a lot about mindset in my coaching, and the *School of Chocolate* made me think about what makes up a mindset and how we change it.

People often say your mindset is your decision. It is, and your mindset is a decision that is influenced by your current situation, past experience, your resiliency, self-confidence, health, the people you surround yourself with, your goals, activities, the music you listen to, the media you consume, and other factors.

Changing even one of these can help to change your mindset!

My invitation to you is to watch *School of Chocolate* on Netflix and pay attention to your mindset.

Journaling Questions and Activity:

1. How important is your mindset to your well-being?
2. What are the biggest factors that impact your mindset?
3. Who in your life has a consistently positive mindset?
4. Activity: Ask them if they are intentional about maintaining a positive mindset and what they do to get and maintain it.
5. How do you or can you change your mindset?

CONSIDERATIONS ON A POSITIVE MINDSET...

*"Positive thinking will let you do every-
thing better than negative thinking
will...."*
~Zig Ziglar

*"We are shaped by our thoughts, we be-
come what we think."*
~Gautama Buddha

*"The happiness of your life depends upon
the quality of your thoughts."*
~Marcus Aurelius

#46

Soul Soother

Our family choosing the perfect tree

 **HOW ABOUT THIS ONE?"**

I felt a settling in my body—a familiarity. Wonderfully green and perfectly full, everyone agreed, that this one was the best Christmas tree.

Our tradition of visiting Bachman's the Saturday before Thanksgiving to choose the perfect Christmas tree was complete. It would be decorated that night at our annual Christmas party.

This was the start of our 32nd annual tree trimming Christmas party. It is a Perry family tradition.

Yet, our annual party has seen changes with Covid.

Our tree trimming party, which was bursting with laughter and love of over 75 people in 2019, was reduced to 8 in 2020.

This year, 2021, with vaccines, we added framily members for a party of 15. For clarification, 'framily' includes friends that have become a part of our family.

Yet even with 60 fewer people, the party was still filled with laughter and love. There was a definite familiarity of joy as framily arrived with hugs and kisses.

The familiarity continued, with the menu including fried chicken, chop-chop salad, chicken crescent puffs, bacon-wrapped pretzels, chocolate chip cookies, truffles, and sweet pecans. Brandy slushes, wine, and beer quenched thirsts.

With everyone full and happy, we made our way downstairs for the "kids" to decorate the tree. The youngest "kid" this year was 21.

There was a wonderful ritual as each one chose their favorite ornament to hang on the tree. These kids have hung these ornaments *every* year of their lives. They laughed and reminisced about past parties.

The familiarity, the ritual, was soothing the souls of both the older adults as well as the younger adults. This Christmas party, which is a tradition, took on a deeper meaning for me this year. One that not only made me happy, but this year it soothed my soul like a salve soothes a wound.

Of course, I had to Google this new awareness, "Why are rituals and traditions soothing to the soul?" The answer was there and as expected, there was a neurological explanation!

Countless studies have shown that rituals and traditions decrease anxiety and stress. There is a certainty in rituals and traditions that the brain loves. With this certainty comes calmness. Our brains are freed from anxiety and fear.

In the past two years, with Covid, our worlds have been turned upside down in many ways. Some certainties have disappeared and have been replaced with uncertainty, fear, and stress. We are, in what scientists refer to as "amygdala hijack." In other words, our limbic system, where our amygdala lives has gone into a perpetual fight, flight, or freeze mode.

So, it's no wonder that in the past two years of uncertainty, the familiarity and tradition of our Christmas party have become even more important to create soothing and joy in our framilys' lives. My soul was soothed on Saturday night, and it continues as I write this.

My wish is that we all find those traditions and rituals that can take us out of amygdala hijack and into some certainty to soothe our souls.

Journaling Questions:

1. What traditions do you have in your family that soothes your soul?
2. What rituals do you perform that soothe your soul? E.g. Medition, chanting, prayer, etc.
3. How can you do/have more of rituals and/or traditions in your life?
4. When are you most likely to be in flight/fight or freeze mode/amygdala hijack?
5. What do you do to get out of amygdala hijack?
6. Could you use any rituals or memories of traditions to help?

CONSIDERATIONS

ON TRADITIONS/RITUALS...

"Traditions touch us, they connect us, and they expand us."
~Rita Barreto Craig

"We not only nurture our sacred relationships through ritual, but we are nurtured by them as well. In ritual, we move, and we are moved."
~Alison Leigh Lilly

"Traditions and Rituals give us certainty. They soothe our minds and souls."
~Trish Perry

#47
Action Figures

WHO DIDN'T ENJOY ACTION FIGURES AS A KID? My favorite action figures were actually my sister Margaret's, not my own.

She would leave for school, and I would cry until my mom said, "Oh, Patricia Ann, you're makin' me right crazy. Go ahead." That was Southern speak for "I give up."

I'd mainly played with the Barbies. Yes, I consider Barbies action figures!

I'd cut their hair and color them with markers—what fun I had.

And then the school bus arrived. Margaret would skip to the house without a care…until she saw her Barbies.

"Mo-ommm. You let her ruin my Barbies AGAIN!"

"Oh Margaret, I'm so sorry."

My mom chose to take the easy path, to avoid my crying.

The easy path was not easy though, it was harder.

She could have said no to me and I would have cried for an hour; I was stubborn like that. But then I'd have found something else to entertain myself.

Instead, she spent days soothing my sister's anger and hurt. My mom felt like she'd failed; she felt powerless and sad.

And it didn't happen just once; it would happen at least once a month.

She knew what the outcome would be, but, as humans, we are more likely to go for immediate gratification and immediate pain relief vs. longer-term gratification and pain relief. This is human nature!

As I look back, I wish she would have figured out her Power Path. How could she say no to me, keep my sister happy and not feel like she'd failed either one of us?

So often we feel caught between a rock and a hard place, and we choose the seemingly easier path because we know that path. There is less resistance on this path, and even though we know where it leads, we hope and pray that it will be different. Unfortunately, we all know how that story ends!

"The definition of 'insanity' is doing the same thing over and over again and expecting different results." – Source unknown, although often attributed to Albert Einstein.

My mission is to help people uncover their power and find a path in life to more success and joy.

Journaling Questions:

1. Where do you choose immediate gratification/pain relief vs. longer-term gratification/pain relief?
2. What are the results of that choice?
3. What could you do to hold off for longer-term gratification or pain relief?
4. How would this impact you if you could wait for longer-term gratification or pain relief?
5. What is one way you could try this?

#48
SNOW!

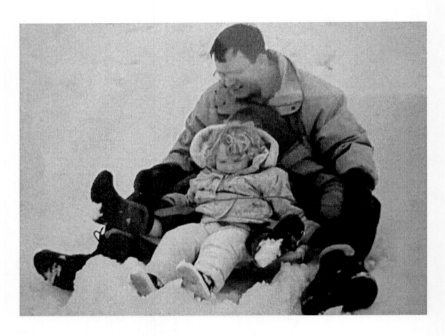

Jay, Hannah, and Riley sledding on the first snow

THIS WEEKEND WE HAD OUR FIRST SNOWFALL IN MINNEAPOLIS. I WAS AT COSTCO.

On one side of me, a woman grumbled, "Oh great, now all of the crazy drivers will come out. I hate the snow."

Then, on the other side, I heard a child exclaim, "Mama, look, it's snowing! Can we go home and make a snowman?" Her mom smiled, "Wow, I love the snow. I can't wait to make a snowman with you!"

When I say "snow," what images do you see?

- I see my three kids sticking out their tongues, trying to catch snowflakes.
- I see my kids dropping into the deep snow to make snow angels. They are giggling and trying to get up without leaving footprints on their angels.
- I see Jay sledding down a hill with my kids laughing and the kids exclaiming, "can we go again?" They trudge back up the hill for the 20th time, never tiring.

- I see my three kids standing back and looking proudly at the snowman they built, not seeing the grass and dirt mixed in, or the cockeyed eyes and mouth. They see a masterpiece!
- I see my kids blowing on their hot chocolate and asking for more mini marshmallows.

The two reactions to snow I heard at Costco were diametrically opposed. I love the quote below and find it to be very true.

"If you choose not to find joy in the snow, you will have less joy in your life but still the same amount of snow." ~Author unknown

This is true not only about snow, but it is really about our mindset in our whole lives.

I had a tough couple of months when it seemed like I just couldn't catch a break. I created a narrative about each of my situations. Those narratives created a depression and a sadness that I don't want in my life.

I want the joy of snow!

I'm not saying it is easy; in fact, it is really hard. I am not saying that I won't slip back into feeling sorry for myself and feeling bad. But at the end of the day, I can pick myself up and find joy in my day. I want to attract joy versus pushing it away.

Here are some things that I am doing to find this joy; I write three things I am grateful for each day; I watch videos of babies laughing, I give someone a compliment, I buy someone's coffee or even their lunch, I let someone go in front of me in line, I make soup for my friends and family when they are sick, and I coach my clients.

I am trying to bring joy to others, and you know what? I end up experiencing joy myself.

So, I am deciding to choose joy over discontent. What will you choose?

Journaling Questions and Activity:

1. Where do you experience joy in your life? It can be anything. Make a list!
2. How often do you experience those things that bring you joy?
3. What could you do to experience joy more in your life?
4. What commitment will you make to bring more joy into your life, to choose joy over discontent?

#49
I Am SO Lazy!

"Self-compassion is simply giving the same kindness to ourselves that we would give to others."
~Christopher Germer

AMOMENT TO TALK ABOUT SELF-COMPASSION from a woman who is trying to break the cycle of self-deprecation?

In 2019 I started feeling really out of shape. I couldn't walk around the lake anymore; I would be out of breath quickly. It made me not want to socialize as much as before.

In fact, we have a wonderful neighborhood that gathers most nights to socialize. The kids play games, jump on the trampoline and squeal with laughter. The adults talk about current events, play pickleball or just hang out and relax. It is a wonderful time and I had no desire to join in.

I thought, *what is wrong with me? I am getting so old so quickly.*

And it got worse. Walking up our three front steps increased my heart rate as if I had just run a mile. I started napping for two hours in the afternoon, and then I started to get physically sick one or two times a week.

Jay wanted me to go to the doctor, but instead, I just beat myself up, with messages like, "I am SO lazy! What is wrong with me?"

"I'm so tired all of the time, I don't exercise, I don't want to socialize. I'm acting like I'm eighty."

Actually, most 80-year-olds would pass me in the mall because I was walking so slowly.

At an oncology appointment I offhandedly mentioned that I was getting sick twice a week. My doctor gave me an odd look and said, "Trish, you realize that this is not normal?" My response? "Well, it came on so slowly that it became my new normal."

After seeing a GI doctor, it was confirmed that it wasn't normal after all. 95% of my stomach was in my chest cavity, keeping company with my heart and lungs. I had a major hiatal hernia causing my lungs and heart to be compromised.

So, it wasn't my fault? I wasn't "so lazy" or "getting so old"? There was a physical reason that required surgery.

My default assumption in the past was usually that things were my fault and I was doing something wrong.

I share this with you to demonstrate what a lack of self-compassion can do. Self-deprecation is unhealthy for the body, mind, and spirit. I am living proof!

I have created a tool that is very helpful for both my clients and myself simply called, the "Self-Compassion Method."

On a sheet of paper, write out the situation and outcome. Answer these questions, 1) What are the facts? 2) What is the story I am making up? 2) Based on the facts, not the story, what is my responsibility? 3) Where am I "blaming" myself? 4) Be aware of the self-blame. Can I separate myself from it? 5) What can I do to rectify the situation? 6) Take five deep breaths and repeat a mantra like, "I'm not the story I make up. I'm enough and don't need to be perfect."

My hope for all of us is that we can be kinder to ourselves *and* to each other! Please practice self-compassion.

Journaling Questions and Activity:

1. In what situations do you blame yourself vs. looking at other possible reasons for the situation?
2. What is the result? How do you feel?
3. Use the Self-Compassion tool I shared
4. How could you have practiced self-compassion?
5. How do you practice self-compassion now?
6. Put your right hand over your heart and your left hand on top of your right. Close your eyes and take several deep breaths saying, "I am worthy and I will be gentle and loving with myself." Or choose another affirmation for self-compassion

#50

An Act of Kindness
for The Colonel

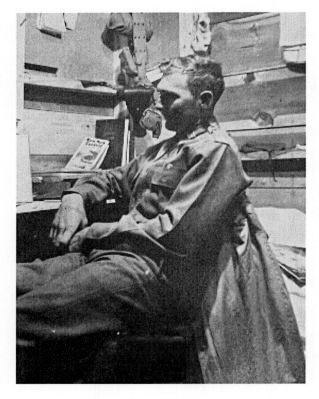

The Early Army Years

THIS IS MY FATHER, COLONEL ALVIN FRANK.
Born in 1921, he served in World War II and the Korean War. A full-bird colonel, he was highly decorated, including a silver star, bronze star, two purple hearts, and many other meritorious medals.

He rarely talked about his time in the military. But in third grade, while writing a book report about him, I found out that he led a unit that liberated Dachau Concentration Camp.

My dad was a true hero.

He was a hero who treated his kids like his troops. His expectations were extremely high, and he rarely showed emotion or gentleness toward us. He was not raised that way. And there was a small issue called PTSD that wasn't even a mental health diagnosis until 1980.

In seventh grade, I proudly showed him my first report card with grades. Beaming, I said, "Look Dad, I got straight A's."

His response? "What, Patricia Ann, you couldn't get straight A+'s?"

I took my report card and skulked away to my room in tears.

Mom told me later how proud he was and he thought he was being funny with his response.

And so it went, my mom, interpreting for my dad to their children.

My mom was the only one who could soften my dad. And when she died unexpectedly in 1996, a big part of my dad died with her. He was lost.

20 years later, Dad went into assisted living at age 94 and into memory care at age 95.

We received one of our greatest gifts in the memory care unit.

With dementia setting in, my dad would often revert back to his military days. He'd show up in the memory care unit director's office and spend the morning dictating military letters to her.

She would do her work on her computer, but periodically she'd stop and say, "I'm sorry Colonel, I missed that." He would softly scold her for not paying attention and repeat himself.

This went on for three months until he died on March 6, 2017.

This director allowed my dad the dignity to become The Colonel again. She made him feel useful and proud again. I will be *forever* grateful to her.

I often wish I would have told her how much she impacted my dad. I think she knew, but I don't think she knew how much she impacted me.

If I could send her a message today, I'd say, "Thank you for making my dad feel like The Colonel again! You gave him respect and love at a time when he was very vulnerable, and I am forever grateful. You gave him purpose."

I often use her generous act of kindness as an example with my coaching clients when discussing purpose. I've told her story hundreds of times, and it's touched each of my clients' lives.

If I had to guess, her purpose as a nurse was to heal, but she found ways outside of pure nursing to do that. She gave my dad back his purpose and pride for a few hours each day which helped him heal in those moments.

Journaling Questions:

1. What acts of kindness have impacted your life?
2. What acts of kindness have you extended to others?
3. How did those acts of kindness impact others?
4. Thinking about your purpose, how do you incorporate acts of kindness?
5. How can you incorporate more acts of kindness in your life?

#51
If I Could Turn Back Time

My Senior picture

IN 1989, CHER MUSED, "IF I COULD TURN BACK TIME."
If I could, I wouldn't.
I'd never go back to my teen years—too much angst and peer pressure.

I wouldn't go back to my 20s—too much competition with myself on who I would become.

I wouldn't go back to my 30s—this is when my mom died and when my hyper-achiever was on overdrive.

I wouldn't go back to my 40s—some good things happened, but I reached an emotional crisis, got laid off, got breast cancer, and my sister died, as well as a few other good friends.

I love my 50s! I am doing what I was called to do; helping people to find their inner power and joy. Did I tell you that I love my 50s?

Last week, a client texted me that she got her dream job. Last month a client wrote me an email that her entire life had changed for the better and she was finally happy. Six months ago, a CEO client went from not wanting to get out of bed every day to finding his inner spark and power, living a joy-filled life which he had never done.

Those stories fulfill my purpose! My clients, my family, my friends, and my connections fulfill my purpose.

And, I didn't uncover my purpose until my 50s.

Honestly, no one had ever posed the question of my purpose to me. I thought only people like Gandhi, Mother Theresa, and maybe Oprah had a true purpose.

Today I know that is not true.

Today, in my 50s, I am crystal clear on my purpose; to be a transformist helping people find their true potential and power, passing their energy onto others creating a magnification of positivity in the world.

So, I am grateful for my teens, 20s, 30s, and 40s because they lead me to my clarity of purpose.

Do I wish I could change some things in my life and do them over?

Initially, I'd say yes, but I really have to say no. Every mistake, every adversity, every failure, has taught me something that has made my life richer, and for that I say, "No, I don't want a do-over. I don't want to turn back time."

Let go of the past, but keep the lessons it taught you.
~Chiara Gizzi

Journaling Questions:

1. If you could turn back time, would you?
2. What situations would you change?
3. What did you learn from those situations?
4. How do you or could you use those learnings in your life now?
5. We can't turn back time, so how can you live your purpose now and in the future?

#52
The Making of a 'Zen Mom'

WHEN WE LEFT OUR HEROINE IN THE FIRST STORY, the Corporate Badass Mom—CBAM—my son and his friends clearly knew the *click, click, click* of my purposeful walk as my heels hit the concrete of the high school floor.

As a CBAM, I was in control and in charge on the outside. Conversely, I was one ball of stress on the inside.

What does one internal ball of stress feel like? For me, it felt like I was in the middle of a lake without a life preserver. I was treading water and constantly fighting to stay afloat. I inevitably started to sink. When I resurfaced, there was a bouy. I would start to breathe a sigh of relief and then the big waves would hit. Big waves were things like my mom's death or even a failed project. Once again, I was under the water and would surface gasping for air. And so it went, my corporate lake dance, my ball of internal stress.

Why did you stay in corporate, you ask? Because I was a CBAM. It was my identity; it was expected of me and I didn't know how else to be. I also had a small thing called imposter syndrome. I was amazed every time I got promoted or was given an award. *Wow, I fooled them*, I would think deep down. And I was always waiting for them to find out that I wasn't really as good as they thought.

Imagine, living like this for over 20 years and never feeling like you are good enough.

But I soldiered on like the CBAM I thought I was supposed to be. Through the waves that should have knocked me out; taking my mom off life support, bad bosses, a layoff, unfair practices, and what I now know were inappropriate comments and touching by powerful men, I kept going.

I continued on like this until I got breast cancer. There was a difference in me after my surgery. It was like time was standing still and I didn't want to soldier anymore, but I was still a CBAM.

And there were so many inappropriate things that were said about my cancer. The best was when my boss commented that the six weeks I spent recovering from having both of my breasts removed "must have been nice, having six weeks off to do nothing but watch TV and read books."

What? I wanted to say, "Well, if you think it was so great, why don't you go have both of your testicles removed and let me know how great that is!" But I didn't. I tried to continue my CBAM persona.

Then came the day I found out my sister had been diagnosed with stage 4 cancer. I quit my job, had my own surgery and two days later drove to Chicago to be with her. She died eight weeks later.

Thus, began my journey to a 'Zen Mom'. I started to realize what was really important. A few years after I quit my corporate job, I received my coaching certification. It was through an amazing school called Learning Journeys (what a strangely appropriate name), run by a mother-daughter team, Ruthie Godfrey and Jennie Antolak. These women help me to take a drastic turn in my life.

I shed The CBAM veneer and underneath was the real 'Zen Mom' that I was meant to be. I talk *with* my husband and kids now, not *at* them. I understand my values, not someone else's. I'm doing what *I* want to do, not what others expect of me. I wear the title my son gave me of 'Zen Mom' proudly because I've found my center, my power. I found the path to bring joy into my life. I call it the Power Path. This is also how I coach others; to find their Power Path in life.

My wish for each of you is that you find your own Power Path in life and live your life with abundant joy!

Journaling Questions and Activity:

1. Is there a situation in your life that has profoundly changed you? What is it? How has it changed you?
2. Write your story of change. What prompted it, how did you change?
3. Are there other changes you want to make in your life?
4. What are they and what difference would it make if you made those changes?
5. Create *your* Power Path to abundant joy.

My Destination

Thank you for reading my stories about my life's journey to my destination, which is still unfolding.

Real, Raw, & Relatable has been a journey from the heart. It is my journey from the Corporate Badass Mom to 'Zen Mom', and I continue to evolve.

Honestly, I never envisioned writing a book, yet here it is, in your hands.

I wrote this book for you, my readers, to normalize things like grief, self-criticism, fear, perfectionism, failure, and shame. As well as celebrating things like love, joy, growth, self-compassion, strength, and mindset.

My hope is that you took your time reading, thinking about the questions at the end of each story, journaling, and discerning how you can make impactful changes in your life and create your own Power Path.

Please take the time to do the exercise at the end of the book. You will get to look at your biggest takeaways from each story, discern the commonalities and create next steps to take to bring more joy and balance into your life.

I hope you can experience a Corporate Badass Mom to 'Zen Mom' transformation in your own way.

Thank you for spending time with me on my journey. I wish you all the peace and joy this life has to offer!

Want more? Sign up to receive my weekly newsletters at https://harmonizeu.com/newsletter

Journal Learnings

Putting the pieces together

"Imagine all of our lives are like our own individual jigsaw puzzles. As we're going through life, we're just slowly piecing it together, bit by bit, based on experiences and lessons that we've learned, until we get the best picture..."
~Daniel Sloss

Congratulations, while reading *Real, Raw, & Relatable*, you have journaled your own thoughts and feelings. Now I'm going to ask you to dig deep and put together the pieces you have journaled, much like the pieces of a puzzle. This will help you to create your Power Path to abundant joy!

Look back to your journaling for each story.

What are your biggest ah-has or ideas you are taking away?

1. _____

2. _____

3. _____

4. _____

5. _____

6. _____

7. _____

8. _____

9. _____

10. _____

11. _____

12. _____

13. _____

14. _____

15. _____

16. _____

17. _____

18. _____

19. _____

20. _____

21. _____

22. _____

23. _____

24. _____

25. _____

26. _____

27. _____

28. _____

29. _____

30. _____

31. _____

32. _____

33. _____

34. _____

35. _____

36. _____

37. _____

38. _____

39. _____

40. _____

41. _____

42. _____

43. _____

44. _____

45. _____

46. _____

47. _____

48. _____

49. _____

50. _____

51. _____

52. _____

Now, review all 52
aha's or
takeaways and ask...

1. Are there common themes?
2. What changes have you already made?
3. What results have you seen from those changes?
4. How did you make those changes and how are you sustaining them?
5. What additional changes do you want to make?
6. What do you need to make those changes?
7. Thinking ahead one year, write a success story about your life as if you've already lived that year.
   a. What have your accomplishments been?
   b. What changes have you made in your life?
   c. How is your life different?
   d. Be sure to include your home life, work life, and spiritual life.
   e. While writing your story, remember this quote by Buddha. *"What you think, you become. What you feel, you attract. What you imagine, you create."*
8. What are your next steps?

9. What will you do with the story that you've just created?

How has this book affected you? What changes will you make because of what you've read? Please share with me at trish.perry@harmonizeu.com

Thank you!
Peace & Joy
Trish

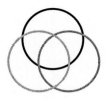

GRATITUDE

I **THOUGHT WRITING THIS GRATITUDE WOULD BE THE EASIEST PART OF WRITING THIS BOOK...WRONG!** Enter my inner critic, The Colonel, "you won't give everyone the gratitude they deserve," "you'll forget someone," "you won't word it correctly," etc. It is true, I may leave someone out and I apologize for that in advance. But, instead of letting The Colonel tell me that I won't be good enough, I am calling on my inner champion, Harmony, to help navigate this writing. Even writing these words gives me the confidence to thank the people who helped me complete this book.

The first gratitude I have is for cancer. In reading the book, you saw my thank you letter to cancer. Cancer saved my life in so many ways. It changed my approach to life, love, and relationships. It helped save my marriage, my relationships with my children, and let me realize that there is so much more to life than hyper-achievement, control, perfection, and the approval of others. Cancer put me on, as my son called it, my 'Zen' journey and for that, I am forever grateful.

Thanks to Ruthie Godfrey and Jennie Antolak, owners of Learning Journeys Coaching School, for offering the most incredible coaching program ever. Your coaching led me to a place in my life I never imagined. Ruthie's basement was the safe space to explore my true calling!

Thanks to Dave Wondra, Elaine Gaston, Bev Lutz, and Judy Zimmer. You've helped shape my coaching and taught me the beauty of authenticity and vulnerability. I've been supported by my ICF community and so many other incredible coaches, thanks to all of you!

To Michael Helmke, one of the most authentic marketers I know. Without your prodding to write a weekly newsletter, this book wouldn't have been written. You convinced me I could write and relate to my audience in a unique way. You and Chris gave feedback on every newsletter for the first couple of months until I could fly solo. Thank you both!

Thanks to all of the people who asked, "You're writing a book, aren't you?" By the 12th person I agreed, I was writing a book.

And thanks to my weekly readers who have provided wonderful comments and interactions that helped shape this book.

Craig Neal, Purpose Coach extraordinaire, you were the inspiration for the title of this book. You wrote an email telling me that my newsletters were "Real, raw, and relatable", thus the title of this book.

Thanks to Robin Keck and Kris Norman for listening to my stories while driving to Ghost Ranch. The book took a new form based on your insightful feedback. Robin coolly suggested that I do not use chapter themes and Kris's idea was to create more of a reflection book. You two gave me the confidence to forge ahead when I was stuck.

I am grateful for RISE Business Academy. Monica Shah, owner, empath, and the best business coach ever, thank you for your continuous teaching, motivation and healing. Thank you, Sandra Halling, for your coaching, motivation, and direction. Your support propels me forward. To my friends and accountability partners, Liz Lopez and Dionne Monsanto, your encouragement made this book a reality. And to all of the amazing women in RISE, thanks for your partnership and support.

I have the most incredible clients who help me hone my craft and allow me to coach them. I get as much from my clients as they get from me. You fill my cup!

Thank you to my siblings Vera Coniglio, Margaret Frank, and Betsy Abernathy for supporting me through my cancer journey. Sadly, Betsy died of cancer nine months after I embarked on my cancer journey, but she's always with me! Vera and Margaret continue to love me in ways I can't even explain. I love you both!

Gratitude does not begin to explain what I feel for my children. The three of you, Nicholas, Hannah and Riley have completed my life. You taught me to love in ways I didn't think were possible. Your matter-of-fact choice for my double mastectomy and your contagious humor helped our entire family to face cancer with hope and grace vs. dread and sadness. You three are my greatest achievements in life.

To my kids-in-law, Kaia and Erik, thank you for loving my Nick and Hannah so deeply. My wish that my kids marry someone who loved and adored them the way Jay loves and adores me was fulfilled with both of you.

And my husband whom I love with all of my heart. You have shown unconditional love at every stage of my life. You've supported me through my Badass Corporate Mom years, through all of my adversities including cancer, and through my journey to my 'Zen Mom' years. For you, I am eternally grateful. With you, my life will always be abundant!

Thank you to my readers. It was an honor to share my stories with you. I wrote this book with the desire that in my vulnerability you would find ways to approach life and ways to enrich your own happiness and joy. I hope my book fulfilled the promise of being Real, Raw, and Relatable!

Who is Trish Perry?

Trish Perry, PCC, is a certified master Results Coach, trainer, and speaker, author, and the founder of Harmonize Coaching, LLC. Trish's mission is to help clients create a positive, productive, resilient, and balanced life, resulting in achieving goals, success, self-confidence, and joy.

Trish's specialty is coaching through hardships. A main tenet is "You are not your adversity." Whether it is an individual dealing with illness, loss, life balance, work-related dysfunction, or an organization wanting more engagement and productivity, there is usually an adversity that needs to be addressed. Trish has deep personal experience with powerful recovery from hardships, including traumatic losses, breast cancer, layoffs, dysfunctional bosses and teams, and business crises. Trish became a coach by accident and adversity; she remains a coach through passion and purpose.

Trish has created the Power Path Process™ of coaching, resulting in outstanding results for her clients.

Trish has 25+ years of mentoring and coaching experience as a leader in corporate and nonprofit worlds. She understands and is dedicated to delivering outstanding results on a consistent basis. Trish was a successful leader at Target for 20 years, as well as other organizations. She works with all levels, from CEOs to administrative assistants.

Giving back to the community is one of Trish's core values. She's given thousands of hours at nonprofits such as Girl Scouts, Feed My Starving Children, MN Council of Churches and Minneapolis Public Schools. She has served as president of the International Coach Federation for MN (ICF MN) and teaches Mindfulness Based Stress Reduction (Jon Kabat Zinn) to teens.

Trish lives in Minneapolis with her husband Jay, of 30+ years, their three wonderful children, son-in-law, daughter-in-law, and three dogs. Traveling, live concerts, cooking, and love of family and friends bring her abundant joy. Her Superpower is vulnerability.

Trish.perry@harmonizeu.com
www.harmonizeu.com